TAMING the MEDIA monster

A
Family Guide
to
Television,
Internet and
All the
Rest

ST. ANTHONY MESSENGER PRESS

Cincinnati, Ohio

In loving memory of my granddaughter
CHARLOTTE GRACE ANDRIACCO

Library of Congress Cataloging-in-Publication Data

Andriacco, Dan.
  Taming the media monster : a family guide to television,
Internet, and all the rest / by Dan Andriacco.
      p. cm.
  Includes bibliographical references and index.
    ISBN 0-86716-465-4 (pbk.)
    1. Mass media-Religious aspects-Christianity. 2. Mass
  media-Influence. I. Title.
    BV652.95 .A53 2002
    261.5'2-dc21
                                                    2002014657

Cover and book design by Mark Sullivan

ISBN 0-86716-465-4

Published by St. Anthony Messenger Press
Printed in the U.S.A.

www.AmericanCatholic.org

Contents

———————— ✗ ————————

Acknowledgments

✗

Every writer's life is filled with co-authors, those who form him (in this case) into the person and writer that he is. They do not share the byline, but they should share some of the credit and none of the blame.

So I offer here my heartfelt gratitude first of all to my family, who have influenced me in countless ways:

My wife, ANN BRAUER ANDRIACCO, and our children, DANIEL (and his wife ERIN), MICHAEL and ELIZABETH. They are the front row of my cheering section.

My parents, DAN and the late JEWEL ANDRIACCO, and my brother, TONY ANDRIACCO.

Equally warm is my thanks to several individuals whose impact on my thinking and on my career as a Catholic communicator has been profound:

MARIANNE E. ROCHE, ESQ., a great friend who told me to write this book. I did not have the nerve to say no.

SISTER ELIZABETH THOMAN, president of the Center for Media Literacy, who encouraged this project and made important suggestions at the beginning.

SISTER ANGELA ANN ZUKOWSKI, MHSH, D.Min., director of the University of Dayton's Institute for Pastoral Initiatives, and SISTER FRANCES TRAMPIETS, SC, formerly the Institute's director for media education programs. Courses at IPI's Pastoral Communication & Ministry Institute gave me a new view of media.

JOHN KIESEWETTER, TV and radio critic for *The Cincinnati Enquirer*, whose sound columns and articles on managing media in the family turned up again and again in my clip files as I sat down to write this book.

SISTER ROSE PACATTE, FSP, an inspired and inspiring theologian of film.

TERRY MATTINGLY, syndicated religion columnist, who took the time to set me up with a list of key contacts when I first became interested in a Christian approach to media in 1994.

Introduction

———————— ✗ ————————

Upset about the "immorality and downright vulgarity" of modern media, a Catholic piest in Cincinnati sat down and wrote a letter prescribing an antidote for this mess: membership in the Catholic Lending Library.

The date was November 25, 1937—more than a decade before television became a mass medium and half a century before the Internet began to take off.

Challenging a media culture that often purveys values contrary to the gospel is an old story for Christians. What is new in the twenty-first century is the pervasiveness, almost omnipresence, of mass media. They are impossible to ignore and not as easy to escape as they were for much of the last century and all the centuries before.

Nor should we always wish to escape them. Radio, television, films and the Internet have a marvelous capacity to educate, inform, entertain and evangelize—to uplift the human spirit. Even productions with some problematical aspects have this capacity for discerning audiences who view them through the eyes of faith.

As a Roman Catholic, I believe that the gospel can never be received or lived in isolation from the culture. The mass media have become our culture, embodying cultural values, yet often carrying the seeds of the gospel as well. Christian families should approach them in positive but discerning ways. In an earlier book, *Screen Saved: Peril and Promise of Media in Ministry*, I offered pastoral ministers some criteria and methods for withdrawing from, challenging and using mass media as the occasion demands. In this book, I do the same for families.

Family members need to manage media, making conscious decisions about how and when and what—and especially *whether*—to tune in. And they should do it together. Media management is not just a discipline for parents to impose on their children. It is a strategy with which parents, stepparents, grandparents, godparents, other caregivers and children can help each other on a daily basis.

The chapters that follow will give you the tools to do that.

Chapter one analyzes the mediasphere, that media-driven culture in which we live and from which we learn. It offers some general prescriptions for lowering the quantity and increasing the quality of our exposure to it.

Chapters two through six will change your way of looking at media and show you how to incorporate this new understanding into the way you use media in your family. Each chapter employs one of the well-established principles of media literacy to give you a deeper understanding of how media work on us as media consumers, and how we work with media. Armed with these principles, no one in your family can be a couch potato!

The second part of the book gets more specific about individual media. Chapters seven through ten examine the positives and negatives of film, television, the Internet and games. They present specific tactics for dealing with each, beyond the general strategies applicable to all media.

Chapter ten tells you how to go forward with what you have learned in the book and take it beyond your family. A table of resources at the end of the book will help you do that, particularly if you want to get more deeply into an area covered but not exhausted in the present book. It does not include everything cited in the body of the book, just those materials I think most likely to be of wide interest.

In every chapter you will find numerous Web site addresses to which you might turn for more information about a cited organization or publication. I offer them with the same caveat that should accompany all Web addresses: Because of the fast-changing nature of the cyberspace environment, there is no guarantee that any Web site will still be active when you read this book.

Instead of the reflection questions that you might find in a spiritual book, each chapter closes with a series of

Family Dialogue Questions designed to provoke thought and action by all the members of your family. Other questions throughout the book will help you and your family probe media as you consume them. These questions at the end of each chapter are freestanding discussion starters. The questions might form part of your dinner table conversation—and not watching TV while you eat will give you plenty of time for that. Unfortunately, most of the ideas in this book for managing media are not concepts that I tested in the laboratory of my own family. Although we had limitations on television watching, they were less rigidly enforced as our three children grew older. Nor did we strictly monitor the CDs and videos they bought. Still less did we use media with them in a positive way (other than books, which we read aloud to them when they were small). By the time I developed a strong interest in the intersection of media and values, our children were nearly grown.

Other families did much better. Some of the best ideas in the pages ahead came from parents who responded to a written survey that I circulated among friends and their friends, often members of a church community. (Information given about these families, such as members and their ages, was current when I surveyed them in 2001.) Many of the other suggestions herein are the common wisdom of the media literacy movement, but filtered through a particular perspective—that of gospel values. For Christian families, the principles of the gospel should be as important in approaching media as the principles of media literacy. I put the two in tandem, two "lenses" through which to "read" the mass media and two "ears" through which to "hear" them. My perspective is no doubt distinctively Roman Catholic in ways that I do not even notice, just because that is my faith background. But I intend and hope that this book will be helpful for all Christian families.

In the classes I teach on "Media and Moral Values: Discernment for Christians" at the College of Mount St. Joseph, many of my nontraditional students are worried about the impact the mass media are having on their children. Even traditional students often express concerns about how the media environment might affect their children yet unborn. I remember one student complaining about how the morality of television had degenerated since he was a child. And he was only twenty-one!

Fear, in this case, stems largely from the sense of helplessness that many parents feel in the face of the media that are such an inescapable part of their lives and the lives of their children. With the strategies and tactics, family discussion questions and resources in this book, you will be helpless no longer. And so we pray:

> *Loving God,*
> *we recognize communication as one of your gifts to the*
> *human family.*
> *Help us to use the mass media wisely in our family,*
> *moving beyond fear and into hope*
> *as we seek to build up your kingdom on earth.*
> *This we pray in the name of Jesus,*
> *your Word among us.*
> *Amen.*

ONE

―――――――――― ✗ ――――――――――

Navigating the Mediasphere

For my parents' sixtieth wedding anniversary, my brother organized a great party. It had balloons, banners, dozens of family and friends, a live pianist, a wide array of beverages, and great food topped off by a classic wedding cake. But one of my young cousins thought something was missing. "Is there a TV here?" she asked my wife.

There was not, but the question should not have been surprising. For its first few decades, television was the electronic hearth at the center of the family room or living room. Now it is hard to find a TV-free zone anywhere in the United States—or anywhere else in the world. (I have seen television sets in a taxicab in Hiroshima, Japan, and at a truck stop in rural Cuba.) And it is not just television that is omnipresent. Electronic media in general, and especially entertainment-driven mass media, are all around us all the time. They are like a second atmosphere, a mediasphere, so much a part of everyday life that we do not think about them any more than we think about the air we breathe.

Any time from the 1950s on, we could have envisioned a common scenario in which a person each day wakes up to a radio alarm, gets dressed while watching a morning news program on television, eats breakfast while reading the newspaper, listens to the radio while driving to work, reads the evening newspaper or watches the evening news on television and settles into hours of watching TV (broadcast, cable, DVD, or videotape).

All of that still happens, but much more besides—more kinds of media (PCs and CDs as well as TVs) and more presence of media in our lives (in restaurants, in stores, in offices, at amusement parks). The best way to quantify that may be in hours spent—eight and a half hours a day on all kinds of media for the average American, according to the U.S. Census Bureau. And a Kaiser Family Foundation study found that kids eight and older spent nearly seven hours a day on media. That is more than one spends at work or school. But media today are *part* of work and school. Also, much of media time is "multi-tasking"—doing more than one thing at a time. Teenagers are experts at multi-media multi-tasking. They surf the Internet, instant-message three or four friends at the same time, all while talking with another friend on the phone and listening to music.

Too much media is not just a kid problem; it is a family problem. Managing media in the family has to start with mothers and fathers, both to give good examples and because many parents spend more time with mass media than they do with their children.

And the information and entertainment media are converging in ways that can only increase their influence in our lives: With a TV tuner card or adapter, you can watch TV through your home computer. TV shows have interactive Web sites. Action films inspire amusement park rides, video games and fast food promotional tie-ins. Books become movies and movies become books. Video games become movies *and* books. *National Geographic* ran an ad in advertising industry publications boasting: "The Fact That We Can Fit a Worldwide Magazine, a Global Television Network, a Web site, a Lecture Series and 300 Explorer Expeditions into One Package Isn't a Miracle. It's an Incredible Cross-Media Opportunity." No wonder Pope John Paul II, in his World Communication Day message for 2000, wrote: "For many the experience of living is to a great extent an experience of the media."

That alone would be a good reason to cut back on media use in your family. Media are not real life and they are a poor substitute for it, especially for children in the formative stages of their moral, intellectual, spiritual and physical development. Time given over to the mass media is time not spent reading, playing (baseball, board games, guitar), praying, baking cookies, discussing, doing homework or volunteering. The American Heart Association created public service announcements in the early 1990s to encourage children to use media less and their bodies more while playing. Even four hours a day of high-quality programming from Discovery Channel and PBS or the National Geographic Web site—good in themselves—is far too much because of the activities they are replacing. And most television, movies and video games are not high quality. The mass media's appeal to the lowest common denominator in search of large audiences usually results in gratuitous violence, exploitive sex, an obsession with wealth and beauty, and a mythology that problems are easily solved and sin is without consequences.

So, if your family spends hours a day in front of any kind of screen—a TV screen, a computer screen, a video game screen—cutting back is essential. But it is not sufficient. Your family needs to manage media not only by reducing the quantity of your consumption but also by increasing its quality. And by "quality," I do not mean only the quality of *what* you watch, listen and play but also the quality of *how* you do those things.

Think of it this way: Even if you threw out all your screens with this week's trash your family wouldn't suddenly be isolated from the mass media culture. They would still get it second-hand from those who do watch and play. Popular TV phrases like "voted off the island" and "Is that your final answer?" reach beyond those who watch the programs; so do ideas and values. That being the case, it is better to engage the media culture constructively than to let yourself be evangelized by it without even knowing it. Besides, electronic media can be wonderful sources of enlightenment, entertainment, food for thought and even spiritual formation. So use less media, but also use good media and use it well.

Think of your options for navigating the mediasphere as a matrix, a vertical line and a horizontal line. One line represents how much you watch, listen or play. The other represents how good the media productions you consume are and how good you are at "reading" them with an awareness of their meanings, values and viewpoints. If you were to put a dot on that matrix representing your own relationship with mass media, where would it be? Where would it be for your spouse? Your children? The worst place to be is where the highest quantity means the lowest quality. The best place is at the other corner, where lowest quantity meets highest quality. Call that the optimum point. How do you get there? Each medium invites specific tactics. But some general strategies apply across the board.

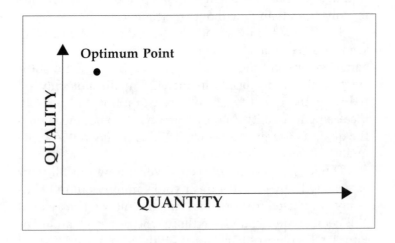

Getting Started

Before you can move along the right direction on that Quantity/Quality matrix, your family has to become more intentional about using media. That means you always make informed, deliberate decisions about *whether* to watch (listen, play) and then *what* to watch (listen to, play). That will set you apart from the majority of Americans for whom TV, especially, is a default option—what they are doing when they are not doing anything.

So your first step is awareness of how you use media now, or perhaps how they use you. Pay close attention for a day or a week to which media you use, how much time you give them, how much attention you give them, and what they give you in return in terms of production values and moral values. Also, note whether you do this alone or share media with others. A media log chart to help you is on the following page.

	Movies including videos & DVDs	TV	Music	Internet	Video Games	Total
Time spent (in hours)						
Attention level (1-10)						
Quality of production values (1-10)						
Quality of moral values (1-10)						
How many people with you?						
Why did you choose this media activity (for fun, to learn, to relax, don't know)?						

On the issues where you are using a scale of one to ten, ten is the high end. Obviously that is a subjective number, and perhaps hard to apply to several hours of exposure that might range from a drama to a sitcom, from *Doom* to computer solitaire. Just record your general impression. This is not a scientific instrument; it is just a reference point from which to compare yourself to other family members— and to your more media-savvy self when you reach the end of this book. To make that easier, let's play a numbers game. Take the total number of hours that you spent consuming media. Now add up separately all the other numbers. That is your Quantity/Quality (Q/Q) Quotient. The lower the number on top and the higher the number on the bottom, the closer you are to the optimum point on our matrix.

Mass Media Unplugged

The place to begin that movement is with the top number. Most likely filling out the media log has shown you that you do not pay much attention to the media that take up a lot of your time, that these media are low on quality and moral values (essentially junk food for the eyes and ears), and that they are shutting you off from other people. Deciding to make a choice about whether to use media at any particular time virtually guarantees that you will do so less often. And cutting down that top number on the Q/Q Quotient almost automatically increases the attention you pay to quality. When you use media less, you try to enjoy it more.

Although a permanent, year-round reduction is the goal—not a one-time turn-off—it helps to begin with a family media blackout. Then when you resume using media, do so in a more intentional, family-friendly, quality-conscious way, employing techniques described in this and other chapters. At this point two hours of mass media a day becomes a treat instead of the deprivation that it seems to people who are used to seven hours.

Taking a vacation from electronic media is far from a new idea. National TV-Turnoff Week (www.tvturnoff.org) gets a lot of media attention, ironically enough, when it is held each April. This effort is directed solely at television and somewhat overstates the case against the tube. Students at Seattle Pacific University, a Christian liberal arts school, broadened the scope and added a faith dimension with their "Technology Sabbath Week." They put aside E-mail, laptops, cell phones and video games for a week to concentrate on their personal relationships and faith. Opening up more time for prayer and cultivating human relationships is just what Pope John Paul II had in mind in 1996 when he called for "a certain fasting" from media during Lent, even while acknowledging the "undeniable usefulness" of the mass media.

Like any other fasting, a media fast opens up more room for God made present in many forms—in your church, in your family, in volunteer activities. When syndicated columnist Father Peter Daly went on a Lenten TV fast, he read the Bible or wrote in a prayer journal during the time he used to watch the local news.

In addition to the spiritual blessings it provides, fasting from media during Lent or any other time will dramatically increase your awareness of just how present, how automatic, and how time-consuming the media are in our everyday lives. "Giving up television made me realize that time is valuable," Father Daly wrote in his "Parish Diary" column. "I want to do a lot more with my life than watch it go by on the screen." He said he felt freer and more peaceful at the end of his forty-day TV fast: "There isn't the constant haranguing to buy things in my house."

As you and your family discover new non-media activities you enjoy, or spend more time with old interests, make a note of them—perhaps with your media log. Return to this catalog of opportunities later when you are looking for screen-free things to do.

Seeing It Through

Whether you are on a complete fast or the media diet that follows it, it is not easy for one accustomed to pigging out on audiovisual media. "When you take TV and the personal computer away from kids they cry and kick," noted Deborah and Charles Siler of Burke, Virginia, whose three children ranged in age from ten to sixteen. "Hang in there a week and they'll start getting creative." Subtracting or reducing something that has been that big in your family life is going to mean a lifestyle change for all of you. There are many strategies you can use to make it work.

Limit all electronic media to a total of no more than two hours a day of screen time, as many child development professionals recommend. "Even good TV or an educational video can be overused," the Silers pointed out. "Lack of these media promotes physical exercise, conversation, creativity and relationships." Jane Murphy and Karen Tucker, in their book *Stay Tuned!*, suggest presenting this standard positively as *allowing* up to two hours a day. This is not only good politics, it is an accurate reflection of what you are doing as a parent: You are extending a privilege, not restricting a right. The family media policy applies to everyone, though, not just the children.

Be flexible enough to allow tradeoffs—less on one day in return for more on another for good reason, such as watching the Olympics, the World Series or a presidential inauguration on television. But do not increase media time as a reward for good behavior. Too much media is too much even when a child has been good.

Some parents have developed or adapted systems for keeping track. "Our system is very effective," said Stephanie Moore, a member of St. Emilian Byzantine Catholic Church in Brunswick, Ohio. "Each week Julieanne (age six) gets fourteen 'TV chips' (poker chips). Each chip is worth a half hour of TV. They also have a monetary value at fifty cents each. She cannot carry over chips from week to week, but she can cash them in for money—an added incentive to stay away from television. I did not want her to feel that she had to use all of the chips in a given week, nor did I want her saving chips for more TV. The point was to reduce her TV time and not make her watch a certain amount."

Set other rules for children's use of TV, VCR, the Internet and video or computer games, such as: None without asking permission first. None before school. None until after homework, chores and any other obligations are completed. "We do not allow television viewing Monday through Friday at 3 p.m. during the school year," said Frances Hennessy, a Cincinnati caterer with eleven-year-old twins. "It has been very effective; school work is completed with no rush to finish 'so I can see my favorite show.'"

If there are two parents in the home, make sure you both agree on the rules and enforce them consistently. "The biggest challenge has been being consistent and not giving in," said Mary Charles of Murrieta, California, mother of three children six and under. "Once we're consistent for a short period of time the kids know it's a rule and stop challenging." I was stunned when a media literacy publication headlined an article "It's OK to set limits." Who would think otherwise? As Mrs. Hennessy noted, "Children *want* limits."

Barb and Paul Bergman, who are heavily involved as media education volunteers at St. Mary's parish in Cincinnati, limit their three sons' electronic activity to one hour a day during the week, and none between 5:30 and 7:00 p.m. On the weekends, there is more latitude for Saturday morning cartoons and Sunday evening family TV viewing, but still limits. And there is a "three-strikes" policy for any of the boys (ages nine, twelve and fourteen) violating the limits. "When they sneak in TV or computer/PlayStation when it is off limits or if they view inappropriate fare, they are simply informed that they get a strike," the Bergmans wrote. "After three strikes, electronic media are off for all (including us) for the day or for the next day if the third strike occurs in the evening. These well-defined guidelines seem to work well—few arguments, and the kids seem to take more responsibility for their actions. It is amazing how creative and active they can be on non-electronic days."

It gets harder as children get older. "After a certain age, the restrictions don't help much," said Cathy Bookser-Feister, a physical therapist with three children. "Our boys just stopped having friends over to watch TV at our house. Instead, they have gone to others' houses, where they watched much worse stuff." A Cincinnati mother with four children and four television sets complained that her older two, ages ten and eight, often sneak to other TVs so they can watch more. "We were much more effective when our children were younger," said Mary Ellen Russell of Annapolis, Maryland, also a mother of four and a legislative advocate for Catholic schools. "Now our youngest (eleven) is exposed to much more because of his older siblings (thirteen, fifteen and seventeen)." She and her husband limit their children's use of TV, videos and Web sites to the weekend only, except for homework and occasional major sporting events. "It (media restrictions) worked well when they were young," agreed Sue Thompson, Cincinnati area pre-school teacher and mother of four children ages nine to twenty-two. "It is difficult to monitor over-eighteen watching habits. They're up later than me." An older parent, sixty-three-year-old Merlin Wendling, of South Bend, Indiana, recalls a similar experience looking back: "It worked through eighth grade. At that point more and more time was spent with friends away from our home." Distressing though this may be, those earlier years are the most important. Children's primary values are set long before they enter high school.

Time restrictions are easier to monitor when you own only one television, one computer (unless an employer or a school requires a laptop), and one video game player. That eliminates sneaking off to use one in another part of the house without parents. Because most children already have a TV and many a video game player, this is a hard one for parents. (It is also a counter-cultural act. Syndicated religion columnist Terry Mattingly once wrote about what a difficult time he had explaining to an electronics superstore salesman that he only needed to hook up his satellite dish to *one* television because he only had one.) But availability inevitably leads to use: If a child has her own television, she will watch it; if she has her own Internet access, she will surf it. (The same is true of parents, of course.) Having these media in children's rooms also makes it difficult to monitor them and separates members of the family from each other. And it distracts from what a child should be doing in his or her room—homework, reading, sleeping. "Our children are eight and ten, so I expect a 'demand' pretty soon that a TV or computer be allowed in their bedrooms," a magazine editor who lives in Arlington, Virginia, said. "They'll be out of luck—both TV and computer use are not to be thought of as 'private' activities." Kathy Olson, a pediatric speech pathologist who lives in Granger, Indiana, moved her family's laptop-Internet computer to the kitchen when she found her twelve-year-old son using it upstairs after bedtime.

Let children decide for themselves how to allocate their media time between different kinds of media, as long as the content is appropriate. They need to learn to make choices, with help from their parents and other responsible adults (teachers, youth leaders, caregivers, grandparents) as appropriate.

When children complain they do not have anything to do, tell them that is OK. They do not have to be doing something all the time. Our culture encourages adults to be workaholics and kids to be playaholics. It does not have to be that way.

If kids have to be doing something, let them figure it out: "Children are creative people," noted a Jefferson City, Montana, mother of four between the ages of two and seven. "On sunny days, send them outside to play," urged Father Mark Hodges, pastor of St. Stephen Orthodox Church in Lima, Ohio. He has seven children, ages sixteen and under. Mrs. Olson tells her son and her ten-year-old daughter that she could find them some chores—a possibility that spurs their own creativity. "They often find other things to do," she said. "We offer to set up play time with kids who aren't in walking distance. We have a cabinet of arts/crafts supplies and kits that go untouched for months. I often suggest they take a look in there."

Make children part of the conversation and activities at family gatherings. An eleven-year-old boy who regularly gives up TV for Lent told Catholic News Service that it is particularly difficult when his family visits his grandmother's house. The kids all go and watch cable TV in the back room while the adults talk about things the kids mostly don't understand.

Do not make videos the centerpiece of holiday get-togethers and children's birthday parties. Provide other activities that everyone can enjoy.

Have a lot of books around the house, and make sure they are good books. (Not all books are, any more than all electronic media are.) Read books yourself. Read to children when they are young. It is especially important for fathers to do this so that boys know it is just as much a "masculine" activity as watching sports. Katie Gebhard, a religious educator in New Brighton, Minnesota, was still reading to her youngest son at age fourteen and a half. Stop reading for the day at an exciting point to leave the child wanting more. Buy books, but also make trips to the library a routine part of your children's lives. Make sure every family member who is old enough owns a library card. A librarian can help you make good reading choices.

Get everyone on board. This means both parents (especially if they aren't living together), grandparents (who are often heavy TV watchers), older siblings and any other caregivers. If you have a babysitter, make your media expectations a part of the written contract. If you use day care or pre-school, choose one that doesn't plunk kids down in front the tube for hours at a time. Let the parents of your children's friends know your media limits and ask that they be enforced.

The Quality Factor

Denigrators of cable TV have a point when they say that a hundred channels of junk is still junk. But it's equally true to say that two hours a day—or half an hour a day—of junk is still junk. Junk is a waste of time at best; harmful at worst. You need to eliminate it from your family's media diet. When you limit your media intake, you only have room for the good stuff.

By "junk," I mean programs and video games that rely on sexual scenes or wordplay, violence, and coarse language instead of a good story to move the plot forward; that shock and titillate, like schoolyard bullies, to draw an audience; that stereotype by race, gender, sexual orientation or other external characteristics instead of drawing characters as real people that transcend easy caricatures. I am not using "junk" as a synonym for light entertainment. There is nothing intrinsically wrong with intelligent comedies or challenging game shows. The problem is not the genre but what the producers do with it.

By "good," I mean good in acting, script and production values as well as good morally. A lot of "family entertainment" is inoffensive but also weak. And sometimes there is a world of difference between popular and good (although the two certainly aren't mutually exclusive).

How do you find the best of the media? We will get to the specifics as we discuss each medium in turn. For now, here are some general guidelines:

Look at the industry ratings provided for movies, TV programs, music and video games, but do not rely on them. Critics of the parental guidelines complain that they frequently mislabel or fail to identify objectionable material. And there is another problem: A movie rated "G" because it has no sex and violence may be inappropriate for other reasons. On the other hand, the Vatican considers

Schindler's List, which is rated R, as one of the most significant movies of the first hundred years of filmmaking. Ratings alone do not help with media productions that support gospel values in general, while accepting some cultural norms contrary to the ideals of the Christian life. (The film *Pay It Forward* is all about doing good deeds. But several of the characters use profanity, and the little boy at the center of the movie is pleased when his mother goes to bed with his teacher.) Other films may show immoral behavior in order to condemn it, not glorify it. (*Citizen Kane* is the ultimate classic example.) An adult can sift the weeds from the wheat, choosing to accept the good and reject the bad. So can older children, with parental guidance. You need to decide for your own children what is age-appropriate, industry evaluations aside. In a sense, all media productions are PG because they require your parental guidance. And that guidance will be different for each of your kids, depending on age and maturity.

Read reviews from sources you can trust. If you do not often see movies when they are released in the theater, clip reviews of likely prospects and look for the video when it comes out. The U.S. Conference of Catholic Bishops Office for Film and Broadcasting (www.usccb.org/movies/index.htm) provides excellent reviews of current releases, limited releases, family videos and older movies, evaluating them both for "artistic merit and moral acceptability." These may appear in your diocesan Catholic newspaper. The office also issues a list of its top ten movies each year, archiving them on the Web page. The bishops' Catholic Communications Campaign also sponsors 1–800–311–4CCC, a toll-free number providing recorded versions of the reviews, including a family video of the week. In 2000, the movie review Web page recorded 71,222 visits and the movie line 89,347 calls.

My Friend, a Catholic magazine for pre-teens from the Daughters of St. Paul, includes video reviews for kids by kids, with questions to think about before and after the videos. The magazine also carries book, video game and

digital product reviews, all of which are posted on the Web
site (www.pauline.org). Click "kidstuff." And *St. Anthony
Messenger* (www.AmericanCatholic.org), one of the leading
Catholic magazines for the whole family, has long had
strong TV and film reviews, as well as frequent feature stories about mass media.

You may also find that reviewers for a secular newspaper or TV station are reliable sources on both art and
values. TV's Roger Ebert, for example, often refers to his
Catholic worldview in his reviews of movies. Women's and
parents' magazines frequently review videos for kids, as
does *TV Guide* (www.tvguide.com) with its annual Top Ten
Kids' Videos List. For reviews on a wide range of media
and a sense of what is hot on the big screen, the small
screen and even the computer screen, check out the magazine *Entertainment Weekly* (www.ew.com).

The annual Video and Computer Game Report Card
from the National Institute on Media and the Family
(www.mediafamily.org) goes beyond industry ratings to
give a red, yellow or green light to dozens of games in five
different platforms based on their content (considering
such factors as violence amount, violence portrayal, fear,
illegal/harmful, language, nudity, sexual content) and age
appropriateness for three different age groups. The Web
site Screenit, "Entertainment Reviews for Parents"
(www.screenit.com), evaluates films, videos, DVDs and
music with families in mind, considering artistic merit separately from the issue of objectionable material (charted by
fifteen categories). The Decent Film Guide, "a site of film
appreciation, information and criticism informed by the
Christian faith" (www.decentfilms.com), offers serious articles and in-depth reviews of current and classic films.
Movies reviewed include some of those on the Vatican's
list of important films (mentioned in chapter seven and
incorporated into chapter eleven).

Look for awards that religious organizations give
to movies and television programs. The Catholic
Academy for Communication Arts Professionals,

(www.CatholicAcademyCommunication.com), annually bestows its prestigious Gabriel Awards on films as well as on television and radio programs broadcast nationally and locally. The Christopher Awards (www.christophers.org) go to books for children and books for adults as well as TV shows and films. Hollywood-based Catholics in Media Associates each year honors projects and people who, in the words of founders Patt and Jack Shea, "by their work have made clearer the Word of God and affirmed the highest ethical standards of the Judeo-Christian tradition." And the Humanitas Prize (www.humanitasprize.org), founded by the late Father Ellwood Kieser, each year honors film and TV productions that communicate human values to enrich as well as entertain their viewers.

Unfortunately, by the time these awards are given the movies are no longer first run and TV programs already have aired. But you can catch up to the films on video and watch your television schedule for reruns of the TV shows. You can also ask friends who are fans of a particular series whether they taped and saved an episode you are interested in—a strategy that has worked for me several times.

When you find good TV shows and movies, tape (without the commercials) or buy them. Build a video library. When kids are too sick to do anything else or want a video for a slumber party, you can feel comfortable pulling videos out of this collection even if you're not going to be watching—you've already seen them all. "We always watch with the kids or at least nearby," one stay-at-home mom said. "The only time the TV is on and the kids are unsupervised (i.e., I am taking a shower), they are watching a video that I already know the content." And sometimes you will want to watch again as a family when you are just "in the mood for a movie" or shorter program. (Many Christian families with small children love the delightful Bible-based "Veggie Tales" series.) Another tip: One mother of two children, ages seven and two, told me she keeps the public television station on while watching videos so that her kids don't see something inappropriate by accident between tapes.

Doing It Better

Improving *how* you watch will ultimately lead to an upgrading in *what* you watch because a discerning viewer is not content with lesser goods. That does not come automatically. We all realize that we have to learn how to read; we are not born knowing that. And yet most people think they need only motor skills to play a video game, and no skills at all to watch a movie or TV program. That is not true.

Here are some important ways to improve your family's experience as consumers of mass media. Ideally, you would adopt the following practices when your children are infants. If it is too late to start that way, it is not too late to change—it just requires a strong commitment on behalf of the adults in the family.

Watch TV and movies, surf the Internet, listen to CDs and play video games together as much as possible. Let these media be the starting point for conversations in the family, not the intruder that shuts off dialogue. Talk about the shows, movies, songs and games. (During the commercials, with the sound muted, is a good time for doing so with TV shows. "Wear out the mute button," TV and radio critic John Kiesewetter tells parents.) Discuss with your family the issues presented and the choices characters make. Talk back to the media—express your own value judgments versus those presented.

Make good choices together. Having only one TV, one computer, one video game player means that you'll have to negotiate who gets to use what when. That is not a bad thing. It is a good lesson that compromises are necessary in life. It also gives you a chance to explain why some shows and games are off limits in your house.

Do not just disparage TV shows and movies your kids want to watch that you think are inappropriate or not worthwhile. Talk to them. Ask what they like about it (if they've seen the show/movie in question) or what they think they would like about it. Explain why you prefer another choice, if you do. Or perhaps the conversation will convince you to change your mind. Make the discussion a teaching opportunity and a chance for you and your child to get to know each other better.

Keep in mind the generally accepted principles of media literacy as you actively engage the mass media. These can be stated in different ways and in different orders. Here is my version, based on the principles developed by the Center for Media Literacy:

- Media construct reality.
- Media are businesses with commercial interests.
- Media embed values and points of view.
- Media all have unique "languages" and techniques.
- Different audiences understand meanings differently

Graphically arranged to present their relationship to each other, the principles look like this:

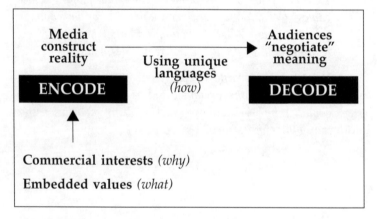

But we could just as well use intersecting circles, for we will see that the relationships are not as distinct as they appear here. For example, some of the embedded values in media *are* commercial interests. And commercials themselves construct reality as much as the programming that comes between them, while commercial interests (the profit motive) drive the content of the shows.

These principles apply to all the mass media. In the next five chapters, we will learn what that means to our families as Christian consumers of the media.

Family Dialogue Questions

- *What does your media log teach you about how you use media? What surprised you about it? How does your media time compare to your family time? How does it compare to your "God time," including but not limited to church attendance?*

- *How do electronic media affect your relationship with your spouse? How much of your conversation together involves TV, movies, radio and other media? How much of your activities together involve media, such as watching TV or movies? How often do you volunteer, exercise or pursue hobbies together?*

- *What can you do with the time you save by not watching TV and movies, not going on-line, not playing video games? (What do you always say you do not have enough time for now? What do you not do that you know you really should be doing? What would Jesus do?)*

- *What is your favorite TV program? Your favorite movie? Your favorite song or music video? Your favorite video game? Why? What makes each of your favorites better than others of its type?*

Two

✗

Reality Check

The latest craze in TV programming, and destined to remain so as long as ratings stay high, involves putting together a group of "ordinary" people (non-actors) who previously did not know each other. The camera records their stresses and strains, growing friendships and increasing antagonisms, as they cooperate and compete in hopes of winning a huge cash prize in the end. In the most successful of these shows, millions of viewers tune in each week with voyeuristic fascination to see what happens next. And they talk about it the next day on the bus and at school or work.

It is a whole genre or category called "reality TV," which also includes crime shows like *Cops* and *America's Most Wanted*.

But reality TV is not real. Rather, it is a constructed version of reality, edited and packaged to intrigue, shock, titillate, stimulate and, above all, entertain in order to bring the viewers back for more. The process begins when the producers carefully choose a group of people balanced to appeal to different demographic segments of the viewing public—something (someone) for everybody. It continues in the breathless newspaper and morning talk show reporting of who has been voted out this week—when in fact that happened weeks ago; what we are seeing is a constructed version of what happened.

Matt Smith, a twenty-two-year-old student at Georgia

Tech, was chosen to be one of the cast members on MTV's *The Real World*, the granddaddy of reality shows. The program brings seven young adults together to live in the same house for a predetermined time, having their comings and goings recorded for the cable channel. Smith later complained to Catholic News Service that the edited version never showed his daily Mass attendance or he and his roommates visiting young cancer patients at a children's hospital.

"What you see is manipulated; they have that power," Smith told CNS. "Everyone wanted something to air on the show that didn't. I was, and I continue to be, a little disappointed that the result of each of our own characters is so shallow and that they avoided some exciting plots."

This is not on a par with the digital manipulation of images involved when a TV commercial, prime-time drama or movie uses people long dead to implicitly endorse a product or say some lines. It is a lot subtler than that. But it is no less an example of media constructing reality. That is what mass media always do, and not just television. They pick and choose to create their own version of reality. Why? Because all of the entertainment media are storytellers; so are commercials and newscasts. Shaping the story always means that some things are left in and some are left out. And what is left in is the interesting, the dramatic, the entertaining. What is left out? The humdrum, the ordinary, the everyday.

Another way of thinking about what happens in this process is to say that media *frame* reality. They have to choose what to put inside the frame and what to leave outside the frame because no frame is big enough to contain everything. Even cable's C-SPAN, which appears to be an unmediated look at the world, has to decide what to cover and where to put the camera. The same is true of Web sites which stream live video or constantly updated photos of some location. Whether a protest demonstration looks big or small on the evening news depends a lot on whether the camera frames the scene tightly, focusing on signs and angry faces, or pulls back to emphasize the small size in relation to, say, the White House or the court house. Here's a dramatic example: A few weeks after terrorists destroyed the World Trade Center, CBS's *Sixty Minutes* showed an anti-American street demonstration in Pakistan. Then the camera pulled back to put the scene into context—dozens of other non-demonstrating Pakistanis either bored or engaged in street commerce.

So mass media always have to have editors, even when there are no actors. That may be relatively obvious in the case of reality TV for anyone who stops to think about it. One hour a week is only a fraction of the tape available. It is the skilled editing of all that tape into a storyline that makes the program gripping for millions of people, perhaps more interesting than their own lives. Less obviously, the evening news is equally constructed from beginning to end.

Constructing the News

Start with the set. The anchor desk, the sports desk and the weather desk at a TV station are so important for establishing the air of glitz and profundity that set changes are often touted by local TV stations. "We won an award for this set," a newswoman once told me proudly as she showed me through her studio.

Ensconced on these various desks are the authority figures that deliver the news. The main news anchors are usually a man and a woman. The man can be older, his silver hair showing his wisdom, but the woman must be reasonably young and reasonably attractive. This has nothing to do with gathering or reading the news, but everything to do with attracting viewers. Along with the sports and weather anchors, they form a TV family. It is a happy family, heavy on good-natured joshing. Off camera, of course, they may despise and disparage each other—which sometimes becomes news itself. And whether they stay in the family is not a matter of fidelity and mutual responsibility, as in a real family, but of ratings and contract negotiations.

After the opening music and graphics—fast-paced, dynamic, impressive—the anchors come on to introduce the big story of the hour. The story may even rate its own logo that puts a label on what you are seeing. (Race riots in a midwestern city became "City in Turmoil" on one local channel, "Unrest in the City," on a second and "City in Distress" on a third.) Speaking in serious or light tones as the story demands—sometimes shifting with almost comic speed—these authority figures usually read alternating pages of the script as a lead-in to a report from a journalist on the scene or "live in the newsroom." At the end of the report, one or both of the anchors will ask the reporter apparently ad lib questions for which the reporter always has the answers. Then on to another story.

Pulitzer Prize winning cartoonist Jim Borgman emphasized the constructed nature of news coverage in a brilliant editorial cartoon called "The Packaging of a Tragedy." This is one cartoon in which the words are more important than the images. They are as follows: Panel one: "Tragedy strikes." Panel two: "Live report from the scene airs." Panel three: "Crisis logo and theme music debut. Anchor tidies up the story structure." Panel four: "Event trimmed to eight-minute news segment. Raw edges shipped to obscure cable news channels." Panel five: "Story is molded by news analysts to fit into debate over shopworn issues and battered beyond recognition." Panel six (a news magazine with the words "Can it Happen Again?" on the cover): "Thus reduced to cliché, the tragedy can be preserved until the next hyperstory renders it passé."

The familiar conventions of the evening news, reproduced in cookie-cutter fashion in small and large media markets across the country, are not dishonest. But they are contrived. They are part of a construction that works so well that few viewers ever stop to think that it could have been built another way. News icon Walter Cronkite—often called the most trusted person in America—used to end his daily news broadcast by proclaiming, "And that's the way it is." Most viewers probably accepted that. But the news is not just "the way it is." It is the result of a long series of decisions by a reporter and at least one editor, but often more, working within the difficult constraints of time, space and the fads and fashions of their industry.

I still remember a joke that I read as a boy, long before I began my own career as a newspaper reporter and editor: "Isn't it amazing that just enough news happens every day to fill a newspaper?" The joke, of course, is that the amount of news available is not what determines the size of a newspaper; the amount of advertising sold does. The stories are cut (or cut out) to fit the space, not the other way around. We all know that, but we tend to forget it. Journalists never forget; they live with it every day. The most memorable obituary I ever read was for a veteran newspaper reporter. After quoting his wife about how angry he would get when his stories were cut, the obituary writer noted: "It's the common lament of every newspaperperson who ever lived." And it is.

The news itself is not an objective reality but a constructed one. In fact, news is so subjective that in surveying five journalism textbooks for college students I could not find a definition of news in any of them. So I wrote my own definition to use in the classes I teach: *News is a report of a previously unreported situation or occurrence of some significance to the target audience.* "To the target audience" means that what is page-one news to readers of your diocesan newspaper probably will not make it into the weekly *Business Courier* at all. "Of some significance" obviously requires a judgment call by journalists.

To be blunt, news is whatever reporters and editors say it is. In fact, it's part of their job descriptions to determine what's "of some significance"—important enough, odd enough or entertaining enough—to qualify. Sometimes that is easy. Journalists know they have to cover wars, natural disasters and elections, and they know how to do it. Conflict is in their comfort zone because they know the drill. I once sat in the pressroom during the fall meeting of the United States Conference of Catholic Bishops, watch-

ing on a big screen TV as the proceedings unfolded in a
room below. Suddenly an unauthorized woman stepped to
the microphone and began to launch a monologue of complaint. The pressroom emptied quickly as the reporters
headed for the conference room below in hopes of catch-
ing an interview with the intruder and officials of the bishops' conference. "News breaks out," one of the reporters
muttered as he left. News? The bishops' mannerly discussion of serious agenda items did not earn that label, but
the emergence of raw conflict sent reporters scurrying.

Some stories are harder calls. That category includes
what the historian Daniel J. Boorstin decades ago dubbed
"pseudo-events" manufactured for the press, as when a
group of protesters pick up their signs only for the media.
Is that a story or not? Pope John Paul II recognized this
phenomenon in his 2001 World Communications Day message. "Where once the media reported events, now events
are often shaped to meet the requirements of the media,"
he wrote. I saw an example one cold, rainy Saturday in
Washington, D.C., as my wife and I stood on Constitution
Avenue waiting for the newly inaugurated President of the
United States to drive by on his way to the inaugural
parade. In front of us were groups of protestors, leaning on
their signs. Suddenly they lifted those signs and raised their
voices as a vehicle approached. Was it the president? No,
much more important: a truck with mounted TV cameras.

Sometimes reporters and editors rebel against being
thus manipulated. But not often.

Another form of manipulation is the more professional
kind. With surprising regularity, news stations use video
supplied by news sources, known as video news releases
(VNRs). There is a major difference between traditional
printed news releases, upon which all news media depend
heavily, and the video kind. Printed news releases usually
are just the starting point. Reporters ask further questions,
talk to other sources, often get opposing views. A video
news release can be shortened, but it cannot be added to.
That allows the source to determine the image that appears

on the screen, which carries a far more lasting impression than the words.

Of course, a TV station or network does not have to use a video news release any more than it has to use a printed release. Whether or not to cover a potential story—anything from an investigative piece to a light-hearted summer feature—is the first decision journalists at a news organization must make. If the answer is "yes," then they have to make a host of other decisions that shape how it turns out: what to put in, what to leave out, whom to cover, whom to interview (and then what to quote, what to paraphrase, what to leave out altogether), where to put the story on the page or in the broadcast. These are all necessary decisions, the same ones that you would have to make if you were a journalist. But you may have decided differently because you are a different person. If you have ever had personal knowledge of a story that you later saw reported in the news media, you may have thought that you would have told the story differently. Perhaps even if the reporter had all the facts straight, you still had a vague feeling that the nuances were not quite on the mark.

Most journalists probably think they are making all of their decisions on a journalistic basis that they consider objective. (Is this a good story? Will readers/viewers care about this?) But deeply embedded personal perspectives, what Cardinal Newman called "first principles" in a theological context, play a major role that journalists may not themselves recognize. First principles are the assumptions that we all have about the world that are so basic we do not even think about them. For example, news critics sometimes say that coverage of religion is weak at most news organizations because of ignorance and apathy—journalists don't know and don't care about religion on a personal basis. Interestingly, a thirty-year study by S. Robert Lichter and the Center for Media and Public Affairs, released in 2000, showed that the amount of news coverage in the nation's elite media doubled during the same period that the percentage of elite journalists who said they attended religious services at least once a month also doubled (to a still-low thirty percent).

Even the concept of what constitutes a "good story" is affected by first principles—in some cases generations of shared first principles that have coalesced into the generally accepted definitions of news. Susan J. Douglas, in her book *Where the Girls Are: Growing Up Female with the Mass Media*, makes the valid point that news standards are deeply masculine. "The emphasis on conflict in the public sphere, on crime, on dramatic public events rather than behind-the-scenes processes, on the individual rather than the group, and on competition rather than cooperation all biased the news toward masculine public enterprise," the media critic and professor of media writes. Borrowing a technique I learned from Sister Elizabeth Thoman, founder of the Center for Media Literacy, I sometimes have my college students go through the front page of a daily newspaper circling all the male names in one color, the female names in another. Invariably, the male color dominates. Here is a good example: A friend of mine did this with 22 issues of a diocesan Catholic weekly newspaper and found 546 male names/pronouns/nouns vs. 191 female. Do women never do anything newsworthy enough for page one? Not often—not by those masculine standards of news that shape most coverage.

The emphasis on crime that Douglas noted is a good example. For well over thirty years, the dominant approach of TV news in particular has been characterized by the phrase "If it bleeds, it leads." The quest for ratings has pumped up the reporting of violent crime and bloody accidents. The Center for Media and Public Affairs found that coverage of murders on the network evening news soared 721 percent from 1993 through 1996 at the same time the real-life homicide rate dropped by twenty percent. Those TV images of dead bodies, handcuffed suspects and grieving survivors, not the dropping crime statistics, stick with viewers. A comic strip has the hapless GI Beetle Bailey watching the tube with his bellicose sergeant. "The critics are right! There's too much sex and violence on TV," Sarge bellows. "They can't do anything about it," Beetle responds. "This is the 6:00 news." In other words, "that's the way it is." Dr. George Gerbner, dean emeritus of the Annenberg Schools for Communication at the University of Pennsylvania, calls this the "Mean World Syndrome"— the conviction that the world is as violent as it looks on TV. That is one of the disturbing effects of how mass media have chosen to construct reality.

Defining Reality

That points up another sense in which media construct reality, that of not just shaping or framing a version of reality but of defining what is real. The very fact that something appears in the media, especially electronic media where it can be seen and heard, gives it substance. Hence the always-popular advertising phrase, "As Seen on TV." And it does not matter if what is on TV, or in a film, or maybe even part of a video game, is fiction. "Reel life" sometimes trumps real life. Before George W. Bush had even taken the oath of office as president, at least one daily newspaper evaluated the new administration by comparing it to that of television's *The West Wing*. Before *Survivor* filmed in the Australian outback, how many Americans' knowledge of Down Under depended heavily on the Crocodile Dundee movies and commercials featuring their star?

This is cause for concern. The world of the big screen and the small screen is not only more violent than real life (in fictional presentations as well as the news), but different in other important aspects as well. Who is depicted and how may differ somewhat from year to year, but over many years numerous content analysis studies of the mass media have found that:

Women, minorities (especially Hispanics), and the elderly are underrepresented compared to real life. There were no minorities in lead roles in twenty-six new network TV series in the 1999–2000 season, for example. A year later, the advocacy group Children Now said Planet TV was still largely a white man's world. Video and computer game characters are even more overwhelmingly male and homogeneous.

Stereotypes are more common than solid characterizations. Media literacy teacher Art Silverblatt defines a stereotype as "an oversimplified conception of a person, group or event." Films, TV shows and commercials draw on stereotypes because that is easier than and takes less screen time than fully developing characters as a real artist does. I ask students, "What is the media stereotype of women? African Americans? Southerners? The poor? The rich? Bankers? Homosexuals?" I have never had a class that had trouble agreeing on answers, which indicates that these stereotypes are indeed widespread.

Gender typing is also standard fare. It even extends to cartoons, where it is a boy's world. A University of Dayton study in 1994 found that cartoon boys tended to be active and violent, while cartoon girls were domestic, interested in boys and concerned about appearances. (The study did find gender typing less prominent in cartoons made after 1980.) Advertising for children tends to break down into ads for boys and ads for girls, based on gender typing.

The central images, including those in video games and dolls or action figures, are good-looking and well built, with the females tending toward anorexic thinness except for their busts.

Professionals, executives and law enforcement officials are overrepresented, especially on television. Sometimes they seem to be the only ones who work at all!

There seems to be more sex and there is definitely less religion in movies and on TV than in life on this side of the screen. Despite the success of *Touched by an Angel*, religion remains scarce in prime time dramas and comedies. *E.R.* had a wonderful series of episodes in the 2000–2001 season about a Catholic bishop as a dying patient, but you could watch the popular series for years without realizing that hospitals have chaplains.

Negative behaviors seldom have consequences. On the screen, characters usually smoke without getting cancer; drink alcohol without getting drunk or hangovers; have sex promiscuously without getting pregnant or AIDS.

Wants are satisfied and problems solved quickly, encouraging the often-noted desire for instant gratification that is so prevalent in our culture. With the wisdom of her advanced years, our twenty-one-year-old daughter Elizabeth thinks that perhaps video games that took longer were better. "Many kids today require an immediate response to everything and have no patience," she e-mailed me. (She often sends instant messages from a computer at college.)

Establishing Importance

For many people today mass media not only establish what is real, but also what is important. If it is not on TV, it is not important. And increasingly, if it is not on the Web, it is not important. As communications director for the Archdiocese of Cincinnati, I was on the butt end of a pointed illustration of that. Someone sent me an angry E-mail declaring that the Archdiocese *proved* we did not care about a certain topic. How? Because we did not have a button for it on the main page of our Web site.

And this is the world—the constructed world of the small screen—that is occupied seven hours a day or more by many children not yet old enough to distinguish the reality level of *Barney* from a televised baseball game, or to discern that a presidential press conference is more important than a *Cheers* rerun. How can they know that what they see is not the way it is? That what is on TV and the Internet is not all that is important in life? In the absence of direct experience, everything we know is mediated for us, mostly by the mass media. That is even truer for kids, who have so much less direct experience. The American Psychological Association, in a landmark 1992 report called *Big World, Small Screen: The Role of Television in American*

Society, concluded that exposure to highly stereotyped messages does increase adolescents' beliefs and attitudes about gender. University of Dayton researchers found the same in their study of cartoons.

The comic strip character Calvin, speaking like the little boy that he is, once wondered: "Why isn't my life like this situation comedy? Why don't I have a bunch of friends with nothing to do but drop by and instigate wacky adventures? Why aren't my conversations peppered with spontaneous witticisms? Why don't my friends demonstrate heartfelt concern for my well being when I have problems?" To this long complaint, Calvin's stuffed tiger, Hobbes, retorts: "Why don't you know any gorgeous babes?" Calvin's final answer: "I gotta get my life some writers."

One of the great lessons that parents can teach their children is that they are the primary writers of their own life. Another is to trust what they experience more than what they see on a screen.

The Internet presents a new danger. Anyone with the technical and design skills to build an attractive Web page can present a sexist, racist, anti-Semitic, anti-Catholic or otherwise perverted worldview in an attractive, convincing package. And thousands have. We will look at this challenge in chapter nine.

Getting Real

Learning that not everything on the screen is equally real or equally authoritative is an essential skill for managing media. Do not accept screened reality as your reality without question. Instead, be skeptical and critical about everything you see, hear and read in the mass media. Approach it with an open mind but a challenging mindset. Encourage all your family members to do the same.

In news accounts, try to separate factual statements from opinions. The reporter may not make that distinction for you.

Consider the source of what you see and hear, whether entertainment or news (a distinction that is getting less clear all the time). Does the TV network, movie producer or Web site, for example, have a particular axe to grind? An agenda to push (whether political, religious or economic)? For clues, pay attention to the choice of emotive words. One reporter's "terrorist" is another's "freedom fighter."

Seek out Web sites, TV programs, radio stations, newspapers and magazines with different political views, ethnic orientation and gender bias than your own, and different from each other (such as Fox News Network versus CNN if you have cable TV). In the non-fiction sphere, there is nothing wrong with media that have strong viewpoints as long as you understand the difference between news and commentary, discounting accordingly.

As you watch or read a news account, ask the traditional news questions: *Who* did *what? When? Where? Why? How?* Does the account answer all of those questions? If not, can you imagine why not? If you know anything about the subject of the story, or can find out, are all of the questions answered accurately?

Read stories about polls and surveys with special attention. Note the breakdown of numbers because it may tell you a different story than the headline and the reporter's summary in the early paragraphs. For example, if the response to a question is 10 percent "yes," 10 percent "no" and 80 percent "I don't care," the journalist can report that in either of two ways—"90 percent 'yes' or 'no preference'" or "90 percent 'no' or 'no preference'." Both statements are accurate! This kind of lumping together is done in most stories on polls. There is usually a sort of neutral position that can be grouped with either the position for change or the position for status quo. Also be sure you know how the question was asked—that has a lot to do with how it is answered.

Get at least some of your news in greater depth than five minutes on the hour from radio or half an hour on the traditional TV newscast. Listen, watch and read some longer-form news as well. For real depth and expertise turn to specialty media, especially your diocesan newspaper and other Christian media.

In sitcoms, dramas, movies and video games, make a game of trying to spot stereotypes and gender typing. Does this character seem familiar? Is that because he looks and acts like every Southern sheriff you have ever seen in a movie? How could you change the character to eliminate the stereotype? (Hint: Maybe a sex change would help.)

In shopping for video games, seek out those that require creativity, critical thinking, strategy formation, initiative, time, patience and flexibility—skills helpful in real-life problem solving. Avoid predictable games that require only a quick trigger finger or following the game-writer's predetermined path to a single answer.

Help the children in your family distinguish between reality and what is made up. Talk about genres or categories of shows/films/games. Non-fiction genres include news, talk shows, sports, biographies, documentaries, game shows, magazine format programs such as *Sixty Minutes* and *Dateline*, so-called "reality" shows from *Cops* to *Survivor*, court shows (*Judge Judy*), travelogues, concerts, how-to programs, the TV Mass and other religious programs, instructional videos and educational games. Fiction genres include situation comedies, courtroom dramas, fantasy, romances, mysteries, science fiction, police, horror, suspense, espionage, war epics and action-adventure. What is the genre of what you are watching or playing? What is its purpose? Who is its intended audience?

To appreciate how media construct reality, encourage children to write or at least tell their own stories. If they need a kick-start, just have them add new characters and a new ending to a story they already know. Ask them why they chose the ending they did. If you have two or more children, ask them to write or record their memories of an event that both shared. See how they differ. Ask them why each put in certain things and left out certain things. Note how they simply remembered some incidents differently.

When you see a movie that is based on a book, read the book to your children or read it together and compare the two. Unless it is just too adult, use the real book—not the Disney or other dumbed-down version. Introduce your children to the real Peter Pan, the real Winnie-the-Pooh, the real *Wind in the Willows*, for example. (Younger kids are not ready for the real *Hunchback of Notre Dame*!) Talk about how the story changed. Speculate why the movie's "reality" is different.

Family Dialogue Questions

- *If you were the managing editor of the* Family Times *newspaper or the* Family News Network *on cable TV, what would be your family's biggest story of the day?*

- *What is your favorite family sitcom on TV? How is that family like your family? How is it different? Of which family would you rather be a part? Why?*

- *What is your favorite movie involving a school? How is that school like your school (or, for adults, the one you went to as a child)? How is it different? How are the teachers like your teachers or the ones you remember? How are they different? Are any of the students like you (or like you were)? In what way?*

Three

✗

Show Them the Money

A hardworking middle manager I know was desperately trying to resist her six-year-old daughter's efforts to drag her out of bed early one Saturday morning.

"Come on, Mommy," the little girl said. "You have to come."

"Why?" my friend asked from deep beneath the covers.

"That lady on TV told me to get you."

In the midst of a Public Broadcasting Service pledge break, "that lady on TV" was urging fans of *Bookworm Bunch* to bring their parents to the TV set to hear a pitch for contributions.

The mass media are businesses with commercial interests, even when they are nonprofit. PBS and National Public Radio carry commercials in the form of corporate underwriting and the infamous pledge weeks. They also sell catalogs full of merchandise related to their programming. One book for parents about television, published by a PBS station, warns about the evil of commercialism, then includes a resource guide at the end that hawks PBS-related books, videos, games and plush toys.

But the commercial interest is a lot more direct—and thus more obvious—in the case of for-profit TV, radio and Web sites.

"Television is no longer show business," consultant Erwin Ephron wrote in his *Mediaweek* column. "It's an overloaded advertising message delivery system." In other words, the prime purpose of television and all other commercial media is not to entertain or inform but to sell. Entertaining and informing are means to the end—they attract audiences for the advertising that brings in the profits. As media literacy teachers like to say, "advertising doesn't bring you programs; programs bring you advertising." Each year advertisers spend around $40 billion to get their message across on broadcast television alone. By some estimates, the total cost of all advertising is more than $200 billion a year.

Consider, then, both the programs and the advertising—how they relate to each other and what they mean to your family.

Commerce Determines Content

Since the purpose of commercial TV and radio programs and Web sites is to deliver an audience to the advertisers, they have to be crowd pleasers. Often this means that they will appeal to the lowest common denominator instead of the highest levels of quality. As Calvin of "Calvin and Hobbes" once said to his television set, "Go ahead, shock and titillate me—I've got money!" This is equally true of, for example, the evening news and Saturday morning cartoons; hence the high level of violence in both. News used to be a "loss leader" presented as a public service; now it is a profit center. (Public radio and TV appeal to a niche market rather than the masses, but also need audiences to stay in business. Notice how programming changes to the most popular fare during pledge weeks.)

The CBS program *Touched by an Angel* is an uplifting, spiritual program born out of its producer's Christian convictions. But that is not why the network puts it on television. It stays on the air year after year because it draws a large audience of viewers in the desirable twenty-five to fifty-four age group with good incomes. A CBS Marketing brochure produced several years ago for potential advertisers makes that point: *"Touched by an Angel* delivers more buyers of upscale items than the other shows in its time period."* The brochure then offers statistics comparing the show's viewers to those of other programs.

Flip through any issue of *Advertising Age* or *AdWeek* at your public library and you will see full page ads from TV networks promising to deliver desirable audiences for advertisers. An ad for the E! Networks, for example, boasted: "We have THE highest concentration of young, affluent viewers in television—broadcast or cable." Another part of the ad suggests: "Think of us as direct deposit for the young & affluent." What draws that audience, of course, is programming aimed at the young and affluent. The old and poor do not count for much in the world of mass media because they have no value to advertisers.

The average American sees 30,000 TV commercials a year, according to one estimate—350,000 by age seventeen. Commercials are so much a part of our common media environment that we refer to them frequently in jokes and small talk. Cartoonists use them as the basis of jokes and storylines, confident that readers will understand without explanations. Attorney and spiritual writer Marianne E. Roche, who has not owned a television set for years, says that she feels most culturally isolated from not watching commercials. She knows about the programs because magazines and newspapers fill her in.

But TV commercials are only one kind of mass media advertising. Media companies are part of what I call the Culture Industries Matrix, a complex web of relationships among the creators of popular culture. When movies and TV shows inspire theme park rides, books, video games, action figures, music videos, magazines (Oprah Winfrey's *O*, Rosie O'Donnell's *Rosie*), and enough licensed merchandise to pack a Warner Brothers or Disney store, all of those products in a sense become advertising for the original source. And the original source, often owned by the same multi-media corporation, also advertises them.

Director Joel Schumacher, who made the movies *Batman Forever* and *Batman and Robin*, told National Public Radio's Terry Gross that Warner Brothers wanted to know if the film was "toyetic"—in other words, "is it going to sell enough toys?" He decided that his job was not really making movies but supporting the legions of commercial spin-offs around the world. "I was really opening toy stores in Sydney, Australia," he said in the 2001 radio interview.

In the technique called "product placement," companies pay to have their products used in a movie or TV show. (Remember the Reese's Pieces in *E.T.?* Everyone does.) It is stealth advertising. Several years ago *BusinessWeek* magazine headlined its cover story "The New Hucksterism" with this explanation of the title: "Advertising is going underground as marketers redefine what is an ad and where it runs." The TV show *Survivor* has included product placements for Bud Light beer, Target stores and Doritos chips. The title of the movie *You've Got Mail* is product placement for America On-line, the cyberspace access and content provider that made the phrase famous (and advertised the movie). The Bowling Proprietors of America (BPA) hired a marketing firm to promote the use of bowling alleys in TV and films. The effort has drawn to the lanes more bowlers—who, at many alleys, can now watch TV while they bowl. Novelist David Foster Wallace may be making a creative leap in his book *Infinite Jest*, in which years are sponsored by corporations and named for their products (for example, "The Year of the Whopper"), but it is easy to identify the trend that he is satirizing.

MTV began as an entire network built on commercials, for music videos are merely commercials for CDs. Although MTV now has other content as well, music videos remain the backbone.

So the first thing to know about advertising is that you might be seeing a lot more of it than you realize. Children under age seven have difficulty distinguishing commercials from programs, according to the American

Psychological Association. Advertisers sometimes make that difficult for adults, too.

The 'Good News' of Advertising

The second important thing to know about advertising is that it presents some moral problems for followers of the Christian gospel. Indeed, it often presents a competing gospel.

Not that advertising is always bad. "There is nothing intrinsically good or intrinsically evil about advertising," the Pontifical Council for Social Communication wrote in its 1997 document "Ethics in Advertising." "It is a tool, an instrument: it can be used well, and it can be used badly." The council pointed out that advertising can be entertaining and even popular art, and that it gives sponsors the leverage to influence content for the better. Advertising also can provide helpful information about available products, stimulate the economy, and lower costs for consumers by increasing competition among producers. Advertising can even evangelize, as the U. S. bishops' Catholic Communications Campaign does with its annual public service announcements. Some dioceses have used advertising to promote vocations to the priesthood and religious life.

The most obvious danger of advertising is that it promotes a culture of consumption, buying what we do not need and getting rid of what we could still use. Dorothy Day, co-founder of the Catholic Worker movement, worried about how that hits home. "We are all guilty of concupiscence," she wrote in her book *Loaves and Fishes*, "but newspapers, radio, television and battalions of advertising men (woe to that generation) deliberately stimulate our desires, the satisfaction of which so often means the deterioration of the family." Contemporary Catholic writer Pat McDonough, in her syndicated column "Family Faith," described a little boy drenched in the media culture. For his seventh birthday he received CDs for the sound system in his bedroom, a new thirty-six-inch television (replacing a smaller one), new Nintendo games, PlayStation II and an expensive scooter (making a total of five). What did he wish as he blew out his candles? "I wished that I could have everything I want and do everything I want."

But advertising today does not just sell products, or even just the idea of consumption; it also sells images and values. The Mothers' Council of the Institute for American Values quotes a marketer as saying, "Advertising at its best is making people feel that without their product, you're a loser." It tells us that by buying and using this tobacco, this alcohol, this car, this cosmetic, this soft drink, this cereal, this toy we will acquire the attributes that the commercial has grafted onto it. We will become cool, attractive, popular, sexy, slim and successful (however unlikely that may be in real life). That is the "good news" of advertising. It is radically different from the Good News of Jesus Christ.

An Alternative Religion

It is not too much of a stretch, then, to regard advertising in the main as a kind of alternative religion. In his advertising how-to book, *Mythmaking on Madison Avenue*, ad executive Sal Randazzo frames his trade as a spiritual endeavor: "The brand's soul is its spiritual center, the core value(s) that defines the brand and permeates all other aspects of the brand." The advertising agency conveys those values through myths, symbols and images, he says. Consider some of the features present in most world religions and in a hefty proportion of the advertising offered on TV around the clock:

Salvation. Commercials offer deliverance from whatever anxieties and insecurities they have managed to create in you. How? Just buy this product for a quick and painless fix. Always quick, always painless. (Not so with Jesus, who promises only the cross.) In the world of commercials, another term for salvation is "instant gratification."

Proverbs. Some ad slogans have assumed legendary pro-
portions, lingering in the mind years after they disappeared from use. Who can forget: "Just Do It!" "You
deserve a break today." "Gotta have it." "It's the real
thing!" These modern-day proverbs are startlingly different from the proverbs of Scripture, which offered sound
advice for living wisely and well. The first three ad slogans tell us that we should do what we want and get what
we want (no delayed pleasure here), and the fourth assigns
cosmic reality to a soft drink. And commercial proverbs
stick with us. When I speak to groups of adults, they never
have trouble completing product slogans that have not
been used in years or decades, such as "Winston tastes
good like _____," "I'd like to buy the world a
_____." "Nothing comes between me and my _____."

Parables. The classic vignette-style commercials are thirty-
second parables, little stories that tell us what is important
in life and how to live. But whereas the parables of Jesus
subverted the conventional wisdom of the day and chal-
lenged his listeners to do something hard, commercial
parables offer an easy way out: Buy this product.

Icons. Orthodox and Catholic Christianity, in particular,
venerate religious icons. Icons, from the Greek word *eikon*,
meaning "image," are for believers to gaze upon and enter
into the holy. Advertising presents us with lots of different kinds of icons. Corporate logos and Coke bottles are
icons. So are celebrity endorsers, the mythic figures of
advertising (such as the Jolly Green Giant, Mr. Whipple,
the Pillsbury Doughboy) and Santa Claus, a saint appro-
priated for commercial purposes. (In sharp contrast to the
jolly fat man in Coca-Cola commercials, who could be a
symbol of overindulgence, the fourth-century bishop Saint
Nicholas was known for fasting.)

Cathedrals. Where do we put the architectural energy in
our culture? Where do people make pilgrimages today?
Sports stadiums, most of which now carry the names of

corporate sponsors, would be a reasonable answer. But if advertising is a kind of religion, its cathedrals are the malls. And they are the most commonly visited "sacred space" for many Americans. I recently heard of a first-grader expressing his amazement at his first visit to an art museum: "Wow, this looks like a mall!"

Beatitudes. We all remember, more or less, the eight beatitudes or "blesseds" of Jesus: Blessed are the poor in spirit, they who mourn, the meek, they who hunger and thirst for righteousness, the merciful, the clean of heart, the peacemakers, they who are persecuted for righteousness' sake (Matthew 5:3–10). Other beatitudes are sprinkled throughout sacred Scripture—Old Testament and New. Advertising has its own beatitudes, unspoken but not for that reason unimportant. When I ask my students or workshop participants to name them, they never have a problem coming up with several. Just a few are: "Blessed are the rich, for they shall get richer." "Blessed are the handsome, for they shall get the girl." "Blessed are the popular, for they shall not be lonely." "Blessed are the smart shoppers, for they shall be rewarded on earth."

Gods. The theologian Paul Tillich defined God as "that which is of ultimate meaning." Commercials often assign ultimate meaning to money, success and power. The advertised product is then presented as a way to achieve those things.

These religion-like commercials are not just supporting a materialist way of life; they are offering materialism as a spiritual path. This is a lie much worse than false statements exaggerating the quality or performance of a product.

If we want to raise our children in our faith, we have to take into account that they are learning this other faith from advertising. Kids (ages four to twelve) are major ad targets because they spend $27 billion a year by themselves and directly influence the spending of another $187 billion by nagging their parents, according to one recent estimate.

(Other numbers are bandied about, but the specifics hardly seem to matter when you are dealing in billions.) Children between the ages of eight and twelve—dubbed "tweens" because they are neither little kids nor teenagers—are considered particularly hot marketing prospects: They are fad-happy, often well heeled, and growing up faster than kids used to.

The next age group up, teenagers, is also big game for advertisers. Media critic Douglas Rushkoff hosted a fascinating *Frontline* special in 2001 for PBS showing how major corporations hunt the teen market. These companies are, in the title of the special, "The Merchants of Cool" because cool is what they are selling to teens—not jeans or soft drinks. And they need the mass media to do it.

Advertising even follows our children to school, where they may be hit with two minutes of TV commercials every day from Channel One, a news program of dubious value broadcast daily into 12,000 schools. In 1998, a high school senior in Evans, Georgia, was suspended for wearing a Pepsi shirt during a school-sponsored Coke day. It was the school's attempt to win $10,000 in a national Coke contest. "From school buses covered with ads, to book covers and day planners with commercial messages, to textbooks and other extracurricular materials sporting corporate logos, to multimillion-dollar deals with soda companies, a growing number of U.S. schools are beginning to resemble commercial bazaars," complained the Mothers Council of the Institute for American Values in a 2001 statement. The group of about one hundred mothers, plus male supporters, called for U.S. businesses to stop targeting children in advertising.

That is not likely to happen. Advertisers are not just buying kid customers for now. They are buying an annuity that keeps on giving as youngsters become young adults, ready to spend even more money, with many of their brand preferences set. The "Media and Values" class at Mount Notre Dame High School in Cincinnati had a No-Logo Day in which students were required to wear clothing and accessories without logos. The only exception was prescription glasses with the manufacturer's name on the frame. Even brand-name watches were verboten. The kids had a tough time coming up with appropriate apparel, so pervasive is this subtle form of advertising. "I had to wear my mom's clothes today," one student said.

There is a whole industry newsletter devoted to *Selling to Kids*. It could just as accurately be called *Making Kids Want Stuff*. An episode of the "Baby Blues" comic strip had Zoe, the girl of the family, lying on the floor pointing at the television with the cry "I want one of those! And those! And that! And I want that...and THAT... and..." The weary-looking mother aims the remote at the set. "Ooooohkay, no more TV for today." Zoe looks at the TV in stunned silence, then pleads, "But how am I going to know what I want?" *Want* is a key word: Advertising creates wants. It is both unnecessary and impossible to create needs. Wants associate identity with products—"you are what you own"—and harm the family when parents cannot satisfy them, or have the wisdom not to.

Conscientious parents are rightly concerned about violent media pitched at kids. A Federal Trade Commission report released in 2000 found that Hollywood marketed eighty percent of R–rated movies—primarily violent—to children under the age of seventeen. In a follow-up report the following year, the FTC praised Hollywood and video game makers, but said all five major recording studios are advertising explicit-content music on television programs and in magazines with larger under-seventeen audiences.

Unfortunately, parents who turn to G–rated movies and family-oriented cable channels as a safe harbor from violence find themselves drowning in consumerism instead. Avoiding ads for the latest Disney movie while you are watching The Disney Channel, for example, is next to impossible. And the same movie will be hyped with promotional tie-ins at McDonald's, under a $100 million deal between the two culture-industry giants, plus a cool Web site that kids will love to visit.

Commercial-Free and Commercial-Savvy

We cannot totally escape the commercial interests of the mass media. They are bigger than we are. Nevertheless, we can limit commercialism's influence on us. Here's how:

Be aware. Practice recognizing and critiquing the advertising all around you, from logos and images on T-shirts to the name on your town's sports stadium. Advertising influences you the most when you do not even recognize it as advertising. Watching television and using the Internet, teach your children the difference between entertainment or information and commercials. Most young children make no distinction. As a consciousness-raising exercise, ask your children to log all the commercials during an hour of television—including product placement and any other hidden commercials.

Resist buying high-priced clothes and accessories with famous-name logos. If you have children who are old enough to spend their own money on such things, help them to compare prices and find out how much a popular logo adds to the cost of comparable-quality goods. Figure out what else you could buy with the money saved by buying logo-free jeans and sweats (which may be difficult to find).

Do not allow children to watch TV shows that are really half-hour commercials. These are typically for dolls or action figures that are the heroes of the program, subsidized by the toy maker. Tell them that they are too smart to spend their time watching a show that was made up just to make them buy toys. This has been a concern since at least 1987, when TV Guide ran an article entitled "Creeping Commercialism: Is the Toy Business Taking over Kids' TV?"

Do not buy the toys, games and apparel based on TV shows. Encourage kids to make their own T-shirts sending their own messages instead of ones created to push a product or a media creation.

Watch videos from your video library instead of broadcast TV. Want something new to watch? Your public library may have a section devoted to videos suitable for kids, although you should not limit your viewing to that. If a video is front-loaded with commercials, as some children's videos are, be sure to fast-forward through that part.

Mute the sound during TV commercials. Enjoy the silence or use it to talk with your family. Or make up your own words to go with the commercial. Try to see if you can figure out what it's advertising without the words. (Sometimes that is hard even *with* the words.) If you cannot tell, that is a good indication the commercial is selling an emotional appeal more than a product. Turning off the sound also eliminates the music, which adds a highly emotional dimension to commercials as it does to all audiovisual productions.

Tape programs and fast-forward through the commercials. Or watch programs while taping them, turning off the recorder during commercials so that you have a commercial-free version in your video library for watching again later. (There is nothing wrong with watching quality programming more than once.)

Because you cannot always avoid commercials and other forms of advertising, try to view them in a light that robs them of their persuasive power over you. You might want to get and watch the *Buy Me That* video series. It shows how commercials are made, emphasizing the production methods used to make the products more enticing than real life. The videos, available from the Center for Media Literacy, will help you and your family see through the hype. (See "Resources" at the end of this book.)

Check out the hype yourself by looking at products while you are shopping. Is this toy, for example, as big or fast as it looks on TV? Does it do what it appears to do in the commercial?

Learn to spot and question the techniques of commercials, some of which are classic propaganda ploys. In addition to many other techniques, commercials frequently use:

The bandwagon appeal. "Everybody's doing it." The implication is that if you do not join in, you will be inadequate. Worse, you will be left out.

Testimonials, especially celebrity endorsements. The recommendation of a satisfied customer is fair play. We take our friends' advice on products all the time. But when a celebrity endorser is making the pitch, it carries the connotation that using the product will somehow make you as successful as that person. Make sure your kids know that a celebrity endorser is paid a lot of money, sometimes millions of dollars, to promote a product. "As Seen on TV" is itself a kind of testimonial used in print ads and marquees.

Deceptive editing and special effects. Exotic camera angles, fast cuts and jazzy music make products look bigger, better, more exciting than in real life—especially toys.

Happy faces. Everyone wants to be happy. No one is happier than the person using a product being advertised in a TV commercial or print ad. Whether explicitly stated or not, this is an invitation to happiness through consumption.

Humor. The funniest TV commercials are fun to watch. But is that any reason to buy a product?

Sex appeal. Sex sells, and always has. The exhibit on Coke advertising throughout the decades at the Coca-Cola Museum in Atlanta makes it clear that the world's leading soft drink has always used images of attractive women as a sales tool. All that changes is the explicitness of sexual appeals.

Fears and insecurities. Commercials raise them so they can offer you the solution to the problem they have created in your mind. A mouthwash commercial, for example, makes you worry whether you have bad breath, then provides the cure.

Hype words. Legendary advertising genius David Ogilvy, in his book *Confessions of an Advertising Man*, identified the most persuasive words as: suddenly, now, announcing, introducing, improvement, amazing, sensational, remarkable, revolutionary, startling, miracle, magic, offer, quick, easy, wanted, challenge, compare, bargain, hurry. These words hold strong emotional appeal. When you see or hear them, hold on to your wallet.

Animation and cute characters, such as animals. We might expect to find these conventions in commercials targeting kids. When they show up pitching beer, however, that ought to prompt concern about the commercial's true target audience.

Following a suggestion of Archbishop John P. Foley, president of the Pontifical Council for Social Communications, try analyzing a commercial from the perspective of the seven deadly sins. Does it appeal to greed, lust, sloth, gluttony, anger, envy and/or pride? There is a good chance the answer is "yes" to one or more. Remember the classic Nissan commercial featuring dolls with more than a passing resemblance to Barbie and Indiana Jones? At minimum, it was designed to evoke greed, lust, envy and pride.

Ask and encourage your family to ask questions such as: Who is this advertising targeting? What does it promise, both explicitly and implicitly? Can it fulfill those promises? What is the slogan that drives this commercial or print ad? Is it true? If not, how could you reword it to make it true? (Example of a classic slogan reworded, "God is the real thing!") What are the Beatitudes of this commercial—what does it say is blessed, who does it say is happy? Do these Beatitudes confirm or contradict the Beatitudes of Jesus?

Brainstorm with your family about how you would write a TV commercial for something important to you, maybe your parish or school. (Identify a target audience, decide what you want them to do or feel, and create the words and images that will accomplish that. During what programs would you advertise? What other decisions do you have to make?) Or create a parody of an existing commercial.

Pay attention to what you watch at Christmas. Seasonal movies inevitably have commercial tie-ins, and TV shows that highlight Christian values are surrounded by commercials that attach values to products and use them to sell the products. Better to give than to receive? Buy a present! A time for forgiveness? Buy a card! Need to reconcile with an estranged family member? Use our long-distance service! These types of commercials are often featured during Christmas specials. A better choice for Christmas viewing is to buy or rent VCR or DVD recordings of classics such as *A Charlie Brown Christmas*, *The Best Christmas Pageant Ever*, *The Fourth Wise Man*, *The Little Drummer Boy*, *Amahl and the Night Visitors* and *It's a Wonderful Life*.

Don't buy products whose commercials are offensive— those that stereotype, deceive, manipulate your emotions, insult your intelligence, make those who don't buy this product look "out of it" or inferior in some way.

Family Dialogue Questions

- *What is your favorite commercial or print advertisement? Why? Do you believe it? Do you buy (or buy into) whatever it is selling? Would you know what it is selling if the tag line at the end were missing?*

- *How do you know what to buy? How do you tell the difference between what you want and what you need?*

- *Do you carry advertising on your clothing in the form of corporate logos or other commercial images? Why? Hint: What does that do for you? What are you advertising about yourself? What difference would it make if you wore clothing without writing or images? How would that make you feel?*

Four

X

The View from Hollywood & Madison Avenue

The comic strip character Cathy, a roundish single woman, leads a difficult life marked by perpetual dieting and failed romantic relationships. In one episode she found herself confronted by the same message in three different panels of the strip—"Be toned! Be fit! Be trim! Be thin! Be shapely! Be lean!" First, she hears it from her radio alarm as she wakes up in the morning, then from the morning newspaper at work, then from her television set at night. In the final strip she is on the beach, wrapped head to foot in a beach towel to the puzzlement of her boy friend. "Why are women so sensitive about how you look in bathing suits?" he asks.

The cartoonist, Cathy Guisewite, had it right: All of the mass media are constantly sending us values messages, such as the importance of appearing physically attractive, whether we are consciously aware or not.

Values are those principles and attributes that we consider worthwhile and therefore desirable—what we consider to be of value. The term is often used to mean only good values, as if values were the same as virtues. In reality, though, there are good values and bad values. And sometimes there are moral dilemmas when one has to choose between two values that are both good, as when a prisoner of war can save another person's life only by telling a lie.

Writers, editors and producers all have deeply imbedded values—those "first principles"—that shape their world view and influence how they construct reality. Even when they aren't consciously trying to send a message, their attitudes about what is important in a person, how to resolve conflicts, when sex is right and when it is wrong, what constitutes a hero and what is cool all come through.

So all media productions—from heavy film dramas to frothy sitcoms, from video games to country western music—present values. You and your family have to discern whether the values are good or bad in the light of gospel morality.

Mass Media Values

The advertising brochure for the 2001 Catholic Communications Campaign asked, "Should the entertainment industry be your family's moral compass? Of course not!" Many parents would agree. Sixty percent of the adults responding to a 1995 Gallup poll said that half or less of the movies they had seen in the past year reflected their own values. (The survey did not reflect those who stayed home from the movies for that very reason.) When asked which values they would like to see more often in movies, 30 percent volunteered what they wanted less of—crime and violence, sex and profanity.

In a *U.S. News and World Report* survey in 1996, even 61 percent of Hollywood leaders said TV places too much emphasis on sex and 92 percent said the tube does a poor or fair job of encouraging sexual abstinence. Content analysis studies have shown an increase of sexual content on television in recent years. In the 1999–2000 TV season, for example, the Kaiser Family Foundation found sexual content on 75 percent of prime-time shows. By any measurement, anyone who watches significant amounts of commercial TV is going to see thousands of sexual encounters each year—14,000 for the average teenager, according to the American Psychological Association. DeVoia

Stewart, a sixteen-year-old student at New York's Frederick Douglas Academy, posed a good question. "How can you expect teens to be abstinent when all they see is sex?" she asked in an Associated Press news story. "It's a little hypocritical."

But the problem is not *what* is portrayed in the mass media; it is *how*. In other words, does a production present a particular action as good or bad? That is where the values come in. Consider two movies involving abortion, both starring the British actor Michael Caine. In *Alfie*, from 1966, Caine plays the title character, a promiscuous playboy who sees women only as sex objects but is brought to tears near the end of the film by the sight of his own child's aborted body. Alfie is pathetic and the abortion is tragic. But in *The Cider House Rules* (1999), Caine is an abortionist, sympathetically portrayed, and abortion is presented as a necessary option.

Nathaniel Hawthorne's classic novel *The Scarlet Letter* and the 1995 Disney film of the same name are both about adultery, but embody very different values. The novel is all about guilt, shame and eventual repentance. At the end of the book, Hester's lover dies and she goes about doing good works. In the movie, they ride off into the sunset together. Absent the disastrous consequences of Hawthorne's tale, there is no sense that infidelity is morally wrong. The screenwriter told an interviewer he was trying to say, "Reach out to love." That kind of love, sexual love with another person's spouse, is not the love of the gospel.

The joy of sex without marriage and without consequences is a frequent theme of movies, television, popular music and magazines for men, women and teens. They tell us that "everybody's doing it," and it is OK that everybody's doing it. It is no big deal. The Fox network made a game out of it with the "reality" show called *Temptation Island*, which featured sexy singles trying to tempt four "committed (but not married) couples" into infidelity. The assumption was that they were already sexually active with the partners they arrived with; the only question was whether they would have sex with someone else.

Naturally, all of the hired seducers were extremely attractive. Attractiveness, narrowly defined along the lines that Cathy faced at the beginning of the chapter, is another value that cuts across all of the major media. Whereas Scripture tells us that we are all created in the image and likeness of God (Genesis 1:27), the mass media tell us that only the buff are godlike. Do you know anybody in real life as perfect as the men and especially the women you see in TV commercials and print ads? There are not many—including the ones you see in advertising, for the ad images are largely artificial constructions. Wrinkles and blotches are wiped away by computer imaging, and less than ideal body parts may be substituted with replacements from another model.

And what is the role of these gorgeous women and handsome men? Decoration, often. The person inside is irrelevant. Music videos, in particular, often treat women as prizes in voyeuristic fantasies aimed at young males. (Sut Jhally, founder of the Media Education Foundation, explored this in his 1992 video *Dreamworlds*. MTV unsuccessfully sued to halt its distribution. But a young African American woman working for the Atlanta *Constitution* wrote a column in the summer of 2001 complaining that Black Entertainment Television sexually exploits black women more than MTV does white women.) The buxom heroines of some violent electronic games may serve much the same function, although increasing numbers of girl players seem to be adopting them as role models. A newspaper story about the Lara Croft character of the Tomb Raider video games and movie said: "She is a heroine to girls and apparently an object of juvenile fascination to young boys."

While the human body is a high value with the mass media, human life is not. That is the underlying message of media violence, and it is pervasive. Just a few statistics make the point:

A study of 74 G–rated animated films, published in 2000 in the *Journal of the American Medical Association*, found violence in all of them. The television industry's TV Parental Guidelines has a separate content label called "Fantasy Violence" to indicate animated and other nonrealistic violence. But some researchers argue that cartoon violence is one of the most likely forms to be imitated, and that it trivializes violence by making it funny.

The average American child sees 200,000 violent acts on TV by the age of 18, a Senate Judiciary Committee staff report said in 1999.

Saturday morning is the most violent time of the week, with 20 to 25 violent acts per hour on children's TV programs versus 5 to 6 such incidents per hour in prime time, according to the American Psychological Association's *Big World, Small Screen* study.

In a study of top-selling video games, published in 2002, Children Now (www.childrennow.org) found that 90 percent contained violence in some form. A game based on the 1999 World Trade Organization riots in Seattle awards points for breaking a window, punching out a police officer or attacking innocent bystanders. (After the September 11, 2001, terrorist attack on New York City, video game makers announced plans to purge images of destruction involving New York.)

More than half the music videos in one study had violent images, and eighty-one percent of those also involved sexual intimacy.

Mass media not only tell us that violence is fun and sometimes funny, but that it is the right thing to do in the face of evil. It is even "cool." While Jesus blessed the peacemakers as children of God (Matthew 5:9), TV, movies and video games bless the death makers. Biblical scholar Walter Wink calls this "the myth of redemptive violence." The "good guys" are at least as likely as the "bad guys" to kill deliberately and without remorse or, of course, adverse consequences to them. That is one of the big differences between media violence today and the way that children experienced it in earlier decades. When George W. Trendle created the famous Lone Ranger for radio in the 1930s, for example, he minimized the hero's use of violence. The code of behavior that he gave his writers, which remained in force when the masked man made the transition to TV in the 1950s, included this line: "The Lone Ranger never shoots to kill. When he has to use guns, he aims to maim as painlessly as possible." In the early days of TV, Baby Boomers watched *The Lone Ranger*. Today their children and grandchildren watch *Walker, Texas Ranger*, who exhibits no such restraints on violence.

The rangers of the once wildly popular children's program *Power Rangers* top off twenty-nine minutes of violence (including violent commercials for action toys) with a one-minute pro-social message at the end. In one episode, for example, the multicolored rangers discussed the need to clean up the environment. Which do you think has more impact on the child viewer—the flashy violence at the heart of the program or the preachy sermonette at the end? I observed a young fan of the show kicking family members in clear imitation of the Power Rangers.

Some experts say that video and computer game violence is especially harmful because it is interactive. When players kill, they are rewarded with satisfying noises, game points and/or advancement to the next level. Lieutenant Colonel Dave Grossman argues that this amounts to operant conditioning—the technique that military and police forces use to train their personnel to kill without thinking (as a defense mechanism). The retired U. S. Army officer, an expert on the psychology of killing, coauthored the book *Stop Teaching Our Kids to Kill: A Call to Action Against TV, Movie & Video Game Violence*.

A new game controller called Bioforce makes the virtual violence real by giving an electric shock to a player whose game character is struck. At its highest setting, the voltage can be enough to make a player drop the controller after repeated shocks, according to a *New York Times* story.

Everyone knows that the entertainment media are brimming with sex and violence, and few people defend it. But most do not stop to associate the content with a value system, least of all the writers and producers who create it. Members of Hollywood's small creative community do not write to shock and titillate because they want to evangelize their own values about sexuality and the value of life. They simply want to build an audience. And as a certain level of sex and violence becomes routine, the makers of media step up the explicitness of both because it takes more to make an impact on the viewer, listener or player. They are business people selling a product. But values are inherent in the product, nonetheless.

Beyond Sex and Violence

And the values conveyed by sex and violence, though rightly attracting widespread concern, are not the only media values that stand in competition to the gospel of Jesus Christ. The loud and lurid nature of the sex and violence, and the way they are constantly used to sell programs and products, may overshadow subtler value statements. And that to which we pay little attention may actually influence us more than the more controversial content without our noticing it. When Pope John Paul II turned his attention to the mass media in the document *Ecclesia in America* after the 1998 Synod of America, it was not sex and violence that he targeted. He wrote: "Everywhere the media impose new scales of values which are often arbitrary and basically materialistic, in the face of which it is difficult to maintain a lively commitment to the values of the Gospel" (20).

The beatitudes of commercials that we mentioned in the last chapter are all statements of what the mass media value—call "blessed"—in opposition to what Jesus values. Dr. David Walsh, founder of the National Institute on Media and the Family, in his book *Selling Out America's Children* reports on a content analysis of television shows by Professor John Condry of Cornell University. The study found that TV teaches:

- Wealth is the key to the good life.

- We should get what we want when we want it.
- Happiness is found in things.
- Satisfaction only comes from a constant diet of excitement.
- Personal enjoyment is of paramount importance.

All of those statements are contrary to the Christian gospel (and to all the great religious traditions of East and West, for that matter). They actually parallel the list of those who are described as *not* blessed ("woe to you") in Saint Luke's version of the Beatitudes (Luke 6:24–26). And anyone at all familiar with the entertainment media would recognize those statements as accurately reflecting the value messages not only of television, but of all mass media—in commercials and in other content.

What do the media not value? Real heroes, for one thing. TV, movies, and video games give us lots of celebrities but few heroes and even fewer saints. And religion itself is mostly missing in action. When the program *Touched by an Angel* became a big hit and a few other TV programs began introducing religious or spiritual themes, that rated a cover and a twenty-two-page spread of stories in *TV Guide*. It was big news because it was a big change, and one that did not last. (Most of the shows cited were gone four years later.)

The mass media also do not value poverty and, by extension, poor people. "Poor is bad. Rich is good," Lauryn Axelrod writes in her book *TV-Proof Your Kids: A Parent's Guide to Safe and Healthy Viewing*. "Poverty must be viewed negatively to keep consumers wanting to buy things to achieve 'goodness.'" How ironic that Saint Clare of Assisi, founder of the Poor Clares, is the patron saint of television!

TV also does not value "losers." Nowhere is this more obvious than in the increasingly popular game show genre. Those who do not succeed are "voted off the island" or told curtly "You are the weakest link, goodbye!" Jesus, in contrast, teaches us that God holds a special love for the weakest links.

Media Make a Difference

The degree to which the mass media, particularly in entertainment programs, really affect how their viewers think and act will always be a matter of some debate. But if sophisticated corporate advertisers did not think media make a difference, they would not spend $2.3 million for a thirty-second spot on the Super Bowl. Medical authorities agree. In 2000, the American Medical Association, the American Academy of Pediatrics, the American Psychological Association and the American Academy of Child and Adolescent Psychiatry issued a joint statement concluding that "viewing entertainment violence can lead to increases in aggressive attitudes, values and behaviors, particularly in children." Citing thirty years of research, the four health groups said that:

- Children who see a lot of violence are more likely to view violence as an effective way of settling conflicts. Children exposed to violence are more likely to assume that acts of violence are acceptable behavior.
- Viewing violence can lead to emotional desensitization toward violence in real life. It can decrease the likelihood that one will take action on behalf of a victim when violence occurs.
- Viewing violence may lead to real-life violence. Children exposed to violent programming at a young age have a higher tendency for violent and aggressive behavior later in life than children who are not so exposed.

The youth who commits an atrocity and blames the idea on a TV show or a movie has become a drearily familiar scenario, almost a cliché. Examples include the fourteen-year-old Paducah High School student who killed three kids and wounded five others in a scene straight out of *The Basketball Diaries*, a movie later implicated in the Columbine High School massacre; the twelve-year-old boy who beat to death a six-year-old girl allegedly after watching wrestling on television; and the five-year-old Ohio boy who, inspired by the pyromaniac characters in *Beavis and Butthead*, set a fire that killed his sister.

Blaming the media totally for these and other outrages is too simplistic. Certainly not every child (or adult) who sees inappropriate behavior on the big or small screen acts it out. For any number of reasons, the youths involved in the cases cited were affected by what they saw in ways that other viewers were not.

But absolving the media of all responsibility for imitative behavior is equally naive.

Dr. Susan Villani, a Johns Hopkins University psychiatrist, reviewed the research on media violence, sex and risky behavior over the previous ten years. She concluded that what children watch can directly influence their behavior. In a paper published in 2001 in the *Journal of the American Academy of Child and Adolescent Psychiatry*, she proposed that health care professionals treating disturbed children compile a "media history" as well as the traditional medical history. The American Medical Association made a similar suggestion in a statement in 1996, as did the American Academy of Pediatrics in 1999.

Many parents know intuitively that media affect their children's behavior. "I saw firsthand how cartoon-like shows (*Ninja Turtles, Power Rangers, Batman*) can influence children," said Diane Habel, a Cincinnati mother of four children ages two to ten. "My first child, now ten, was very aggressive and physical because he watched too much of these—and had the toys to match!"

Children themselves believe there is a connection between what they see on the screen and what they do in real life. In a Children Now poll of kids ten to sixteen years old, sixty-two percent said sex on TV and in the movies influences kids to have sex before they are ready (not to mention before they are married). A Kaiser Foundation report noted "the few existing studies consistently point to a relationship between exposure to sexual content and sexual beliefs, attitudes and behaviors."

A classic study of three Canadian towns from the 1970s

provides a good illustration, not about sexual activity but about sexual stereotyping. Researcher T. S. Williams found that boys and girls in a town with no television and a town with limited television had weaker gender-typed views than a town with multiple channels of TV. Two years later, with the introduction of TV into the town that did not have it and an expansion of TV in the town where it was limited, kids in those towns had developed gender-typed views similar to children who had been exposed to more television all along.

More recently, Harvard anthropologist Anne Becker found a startling impact on the culture of Fiji shortly after Western TV was introduced via satellite in 1995. More than four-fifths of Fijian women are overweight by U.S. standards, but they did not used to care. With the arrival of such shows as *Melrose Place* and *Beverly Hills 90210*, however, Dr. Becker found that the number of teenage girls who vomited to control their weight jumped fivefold. And Fijian girls who watched the most TV were half again as likely to feel fat and one-third more likely to be on a diet than other girls their age. What is true in this traditional island culture is at least as true, if not more so, in media saturated America: Media make a difference in our values system.

Keeping Values in View

If values about human bodies and human life are transmitted through the mass media, primarily in entertainment programming, it's only reasonable that other values are passed on through movies, TV shows, music videos, the Internet and computer games as well. And when those values are contrary to the gospel, they can be particularly damaging to youths whose own value systems are not set strongly enough for them to hold onto the good and reject the rest in the mass media. So you need to share with your family the movies, the music, the shows and the books that lift up the values that are important to you. Seek out video and computer games that offer intellectual challenge instead of the instant gratification of the violent solution. For yourself and for your family, you also need to contest the values of the mass media, and in some cases tune them out. Some guidelines:

Pay attention to how the media have affected your family values—what you think is important, whom you honor, what you talk about, how you talk, how you dress, how you have branded yourselves with product logos.

Listen to the words of the music playing in your car—because your children may be. A friend of mine turned off a CD one day when she realized the song she liked so much had lyrics inappropriate for her young daughter.

If your family enjoys music videos, explore the works of Christian artists. There are some writing and performing in every decent musical genre, from country to rap.

As you watch TV and movies or play computer/video games with your children, discuss consequences and alternatives. In real life, violence and bad moral decisions hurt both the immediate victim and others such as the victim's family. Do you see that in this media production? If not, what are the likely consequences not portrayed? Talk about how characters could have acted differently—solved problems without violence or chose not to lie or engage in casual sex—and how that would have changed the outcome.

Do not depend on a mechanical device or computer software to deal with sex and violence for you. Real parental control is parents being in control, and you cannot delegate that responsibility to a v-chip or Internet filtering software. For one thing, v-chip blocking is based on the industry's TV parental guideline ratings, which critics say mislabel or fail to label with the S (sex), V (violence) or FV (fantasy violence) descriptors. For example, a TV-G rating is no guarantee that a program is free of sex, violence or crude language. And if the ratings do not identify a program as unsuitable for a particular age group, the v-chip will not screen it out. Also, the v-chip is a black and white approach. It may screen out violence that you would think is acceptable because it is presented as a negative or an unfortunate last resort that nevertheless has consequences. The "v" in v-chip does not stand for values. And finally, if an adult can program a v-chip, a kid can disable it.

Internet filtering programs also have flaws: A *Consumer Reports* test of seven programs in 2001 showed that all let through some objectionable sites while blocking others that shouldn't have been blocked. The video game industry's ratings system has won high marks as being the most informative, but the National Institute on Media and the Family says that most retailers routinely let children under seventeen buy video games rated for older children. Be alert.

In looking for productions that embrace your values, you might put industry ratings systems into context as suggested in chapter one. Why is this movie, TV show, or game rated this way? One of our sons once tried to assure me that the R rating of a movie he wanted to see was "just for violence." That did not reassure me! On the other hand, some R–rated movies may carry a good message for older teens. The "Reasons for Movie Ratings" Web site (www.filmratings.com) from the Classifications and Ratings Administration allows you to search any movie by name to get both the rating and the reason for it.

The best help in understanding the rating and going beyond is probably a like-minded person who has seen the production or played the game. The description on the package is also helpful. For example, the computer game "Forbidden Strike," rated E for everyone, carries a notation that it portrays "animated blood, animated violence." The package also quotes from a review that describes it as "one of the most beautiful war games to date." Another computer game, "Crimson Skies," carries a rating of T for teens and a promise of "Big Guns. Fast Planes. Gorgeous Dames." As for the women, the description warns, "these beauties can turn you on faster than a Fairchild in a terminal tail spin." The package also notes animated violence and use of alcohol.

Rent a game before you buy it. Play it with your children. As you watch a movie, television show or a video together as a family, or as you play a computer/video game, pay attention to and talk about the antagonists. Which is the hero? Generally, that character's actions— which demonstrate his or her values—are endorsed. Which is the villain? Generally, that character's actions and values are disdained. (This is not to say that everything the hero does is right in a film with gospel values, only that the total thrust is. The hero may make mistakes and do wrong things along the way, but later recognizes the errors and disavows them. The change of heart then becomes a journey of redemption, as in the film *Cry, the Beloved Country*.) The charts at the end of this chapter may help you follow the main characters.

Family Dialogue Questions

- *Would you rather have a popular toy to play with or a good friend to play with? Why? (Note that this question is for all ages. Adults have toys, too.)*

- *How do violent shows/games make you feel? Is that good or bad? Why?*

- *Who is your favorite fictional villain? What does this person do that is so bad? Can you ever see yourself doing something similar, maybe on a smaller scale?*

- *Who is your favorite fictional hero/heroine? What makes him/her heroic? Does your hero ever do anything you think is not right?*

- *When, if ever, is it OK to hurt someone in real life? When is it not OK? What does Jesus say about hurting others and responding to those who hurt us?*

The Hero's Way	
Decision Points (Wherever the character has a choice of how to deal with a person or a problem)	**Values Represented** What is being valued by this choice? How does this accord with the values of the gospel? What are the other options?
1.	
2.	
3.	
4.	

Five

———————— ✗ ————————

¿Habla Usted Audiovisual?

Just as money is the "why" of media constructing reality and values is the "what," the languages of the mass media are the "how." By "languages" I mean the special techniques, different with each medium, that the creators use to express themselves. Only by knowing the language can you read the full meaning of the audiovisual "text."

Obviously, if you do not know German you will not be able to completely understand books, magazines, newspapers, Web sites and other material written in that language. Nor will you understand a radio broadcast or the sound track of a movie or TV show. But no medium relies only on words to communicate. Print, for example, can also use charts, diagrams and photos to convey information. Television, movies and music videos employ non-verbal language to a much greater degree than print does. This audiovisual language—which affects viewers on an emotional and subconscious level—has its own grammar, made up of sequences and scenes instead of sentences and paragraphs. And it has its own parts of speech, such as:

- color or black and white
- music
- laugh tracks
- animation
- point of view (establishing shot, close up, medium shot, long shot)

- tilt (camera shooting up or down)
- pan (camera moving slowly from side to side)
- quick cuts
- slow motion
- fast motion
- other special effects

Different genres or kinds of content use these elements in different ways, just as we use different words when writing a love letter versus a term paper for school or when talking to a child versus talking to our boss. In fact, the kind of audiovisual language helps us peg the nature of the content. The laugh track tells us near the beginning of the sitcom that this is a comedy, not a drama with funny lines. Special effects in the opening scenes of a movie may signal its nature as a science fiction epic or a far-out action flick. Media literacy teachers like to use a video produced by the British Broadcasting Corporation in the 1960s as an April Fool's Day joke. I saw it on TV as a child and remembered it at least thirty years later. It purports to be a documentary about the annual harvesting of the Swiss spaghetti crop. Spaghetti—like money—does not really grow on trees, of course, but in this little masterpiece, it does. What makes the piece believable to the naive and hilarious to everyone else is its deadpan use of black and white film, British upper class narrative voice, appropriate music, and specific details—all part of the language of serious documentary films.

Commercials sometimes use the language of another genre in order a achieve a particular effect. A documentary-style commercial, for example, might use a dramatic voice-over, specific dates, and interviews with participants in a real incident to gain credibility. A mini-musical, on the other hand, has singing to attach a lighthearted feeling to the product advertised.

One could argue that sex and violence also have become part of the language of movies, TV shows and video games, so pervasive and so expected are they. But that is a content issue. We are considering language as part of the form, the way audiovisual communicators tell the story—any story. (For example, the quick cuts so prevalent in television today are generally traced to MTV but probably originated with *Sesame Street*.) This is the sense in which Pope John Paul II, in his 1995 World Communications Day message on the cinema, urged Catholics to "learn the language of film." Just as words embody nuances that allow a novelist to communicate more than just a storyline, the language of film and video (including games) adds to the emotional impact of the visuals. That is part of what makes audiovisual media so much more effective in evoking strong emotions than all but the best writing.

Effects of Audiovisual Language

Consider music. The tempo of the music during the opening credits of a film are a good clue to whether this is an action film, romantic comedy or serious drama. What kind of music comes to mind when you think of lovers meeting? A chase scene? A desperate search through a crowded city street? Some notes probably popped into your head right away and seemed quite natural. A film director could not use chase music with a romantic scene because it would not make sense. The music supports and in fact helps to establish the emotions connected with a scene. Suppose you walked in late into a movie and saw a man grab and kiss a woman with gusto. Is it rape or is it rapture? The music tells you. When CNN Headline News reinvented itself to became even faster paced in 2001, the network introduced an original new theme song with more than sixty variations to fit the nature of the news being presented.

German filmmaker Leni Riefenstahl used both music and camera angles with great artistry in her famous propaganda movie, *Triumph of the Will*. "The film portrays the National Socialist movement in such heroic images you wonder how we ever won the war," says the description on the back of the Video Yesteryear version. This official record of the Sixth Nazi Party Congress at Nuremberg in 1934 is such a textbook of film language that it is completely understandable without subtitles. A range of music from mellow to martial sets the proper mood for each scene. Visuals of vast crowds with smiling faces establish the party's popular support. And the cameras tilt up at führer Adolf Hitler, the German eagle and Nazi flags. Tilting up always puts the subject into a position of strength. Tilting down puts the subject in a position of weakness. Notice how often the camera tilts down on women, even in women's magazines.

Kinds of shots are also important. An *establishing shot*, whether at the beginning of a news report or a major motion picture, orients the viewer to the location and circumstances. Like all camera shots, it frames the situation. A *close-up* focuses in on a person or thing of special importance. It is often used to show emotion and to suggest intimacy. The camera zooms in or a second camera cuts in and we have the feeling of suddenly being much closer to the person and the event. A *two-shot*, in which the camera frames two people, indicates a relationship between the two at that moment. We watch as though we are eavesdropping on a private conversation. A *long shot*, in which the camera is distanced from the participants, puts people (or things) into the context of their larger surroundings. Our feelings, too, are more remote than in the closer shots.

From Oral Culture and Back Again

Television, movies, computers and video games all interpret the world for us with the aid of images on a screen. Think of how television news is dependent upon images to tell a story—so much so that in an ongoing story one dramatic piece of video gets screen time over and over again ad nauseam.

This emphasis on the visual in electronic media may lead us to assume that electronic media have ushered in an image culture. But images have been part of our culture ever since the invention of writing. What actually distinguishes the age of mass media is the never-ending presence of sound—from television, videos, radio, video/computer games and RealAudio on the computer. People who turn on a television first thing when they walk into a room often do not even look at the tube. The sound keeps them company as they walk through their home. Father Peter Daly, in his syndicated column describing how a Lenten TV fast had affected him, wrote: "There isn't the endless noise. Now, when I go to the nursing home or hospital, I am so aware of the television's constant nagging presence." On Good Shepherd Sunday recently, I both heard a homily and read a reflection raising the question of how we can ever hear our Shepherd's voice above the sounds of mass media.

We also talk a lot. Mary, the Mother of God, has been called Our Lady of Silence because the Scriptures record her saying very little. She pondered in her heart (Luke 2:51). But today, even in church, worshipers seem to find it hard to allow others to pray for a few moments in silence before the beginning of Mass. If people are not making noise, their cell phones are. How often have you heard phones ringing during the liturgy, perhaps even a wedding or a funeral? The company Cingular Wireless really captured the spirit of the age with a billboard proclaiming, "Silence is Weird." Thus, Walter Ong, S.J., and others have dubbed ours a "secondary oral" culture.

The first humans communicated to each other only through speech. That was the original oral culture. The Bible, though written, reflects the style of speech and thinking of an oral culture with its orientation to the past and a sense of communal identity united by the story. Writing, invented by the Sumerians around 3500 B.C., changed the way people think. They did not have to memorize so much, and they could write down ideas to be read by people they would never know. But being separated from their audience, not having the chance to answer questions or correct misconceptions, meant they had to be much more precise in their use of words. Jesus read the Hebrew texts on scrolls (Luke 4:18). The early Christians assembled their Scriptures in the first primitive books. Monks in the Middle Ages copied them in beautiful editions that common people would never see or understand—they were expensive, rare and written in Latin.

Johannes Gutenberg's movable type made print the first truly mass medium. When he printed his famous Bible in 1456, there were fewer than fifty thousand books in all of Europe by one estimate. Within fifty years, that had sky-rocketed to nine million volumes, most of them religious. Electronic media did not launch the information age; it was the invention nearly five centuries earlier of a printing system that made the production of books cheap and quick. The late media prophet Marshall McLuhan argued that printing on a grand scale led to such widespread effects as:

nationalism, because standardizing languages in print solidified the common identity of people speaking, reading and writing the same languages

markets, because the manufacture of books as the first mass-produced item allowed each one to be priced the same, setting a pattern

individualism, because more people could now own books to read silently and privately

linear thought—the progression from one idea to the next in progressive order—because that's the way books are arranged, from chapter one, page one to the end

the Enlightenment, that eighteenth-century intellectual movement that glorified facts (that which can be proven) and pushed values out of the public square and into the private sphere for the first time since the rise of Christendom about fifteen hundred years earlier

Print changed the world in these ways because of the nature of print itself, not because of what was printed. That is part of what McLuhan meant by his famous phrase, "the medium is the message." Now that print—although still important—is no longer the dominant medium of our culture, some of the characteristics of print culture are being lost. Most notably, the logic of linear thinking is giving way to the fragmentation of channel surfing, MTV and the Internet. The credibility gained by putting a statement in print is gone. "As Seen on TV" is a much more powerful credential than appearing in a book, newspaper, or magazine. And as use of the Internet grows exponentially, so does the Internet's use of video and audio.

And so we come back to sound as a language of the mass media. Teaching a special Saturday science class to a group of gifted junior high students, my wife wrote out the instructions for a task on a sheet of paper and handed it out. But these very bright, highly literate students kept asking her to tell them what to do so they would not have to read. Television, movies and video games that talk have made reading an unusual burden for them. Their computers even tell them, "You've got mail!" Words are only a small part of the audio language of mass media, however. Music, gunshots, canned laughter and car crash noises have become part of the sound track of our lives.

Watch Their Language

The strong emotional effect of audiovisual language can be used to make viewers feel sympathy for the characters and, thereby, the values they represent. That can be manipulative. It is poor art. But music, camera angles and even special effects in the hands of a great director is language that we should appreciate and enjoy, just like words in the hands of a master writer.

Whether you want to enjoy the best of audiovisual language or protect yourself against that which manipulates, you have to first be aware of it. Here are a few exercises:

During a particularly dramatic or action-packed scene in a TV show, video, or game, mute the sound. How do your emotions change? Do you feel less excited? Less sad? Less happy?

What is the genre of the show or movie—sitcom, mystery, science fiction, drama, action-adventure, romantic comedy, musical, the news, talk show, cartoon or "reality" show? How does the language support that and even identify it? How would the language be different if the genre were different?

How high can you count before the image changes in some way as the camera shifts? Does that length of scenes vary with different genres? What is the effect of quick cuts on you?

In a commercial, what other genre is it mirroring with the language it is employing? Why? In other words, what aspects of that genre (mystery, musical, documentary) is the commercial maker trying to appropriate for the benefit of the product advertised?

Pay attention to the camera angles in print and on the screen, in commercials and in programming. Is the camera tilting up or down or looking straight on? What kinds of people (by gender, race, social position) does the camera tilt up to? What kinds of people does the camera tilt down on?

Family Dialogue Questions

• *How would your world be different if you could not see? If you could not hear? Which is more important to your daily life? Which is more important to understanding and enjoying a movie? A TV show? A video game? A Web site?*

• *How important are special effects to your enjoyment of a movie, TV show, video game, Web site? Do you ever comment on the special effects of something you have just seen?*

• *Think of a story that you know well, perhaps a story about Jesus. What special "language" or techniques would you use to tell that as a breaking news story? As a documentary? As a musical play?*

Six

✗

What You See Is Not All You Get

In Mark Twain's great American novel, *The Adventures of Huckleberry Finn*, a lying Huckleberry tells Tom Sawyer's Aunt Sally about a steamboat incident that never actually happened. "Good gracious! Anybody hurt?" she asks. "No'm," he assures her, adding that it killed an African American person. He uses the "n-word," one of hundreds of times the offensive word is used throughout the novel. "Well, it's lucky," Aunt Sally says, "because sometimes people do get hurt."

That kind of language, and the attitude that Huckleberry and Aunt Sally seem to exhibit in the scene I just described, have made the book extremely controversial for decades. Some people have called the book racist and demanded that it not be required reading in schools. In truth, however, the novel is antiracist to its core. The passage about the made-up steamboat accident comes just one chapter after Huckleberry—the hero and moral center of the book—decides not to turn in his friend Jim, the runaway slave. He makes this decision even though he believes he is doing the wrong thing and will go to hell as a result. "All right, then, I'll *go* to hell," he thinks.

Opponents and supporters of the novel are reading the same book, but reading it in such different ways that they are almost making it two different books. Those who think the book is racist miss the ironic distance. Aunt Sally does not consider slaves as people, but the author certainly does.

Her values and Twain's are quite different. That is clear in the light of the chapter before it and Huckleberry's actions throughout the book.

The novel, first published in 1885, remains controversial because different audiences still read (or understand) the same material in different ways. A hundred years from now parents, educators and religious leaders may still be arguing about whether the Harry Potter books are delightful works of imagination or dangerous forays into wizardry. (Meanwhile, I suspect, children will still be enjoying Harry's adventures.)

Message Sent Versus Message Received

The producers of creative works—writers and directors—always have a purpose and sometimes a serious message. However, that purpose and message are subject to interpretation by the receiver. Think of all the different ways that people interpret the Bible—Jews, Christians and Muslims, and multiple divisions within each of those faith groups. On a more mundane level, recall how you once said something and your spouse, child, or grandchild heard something else. Misinterpretation in the tone of E-mails has led to such disastrous consequences, personal and business, that many E-mail users have adopted a signal system to let recipients know when they are joking and to express other emotions.

Similarly, as we saw in the last chapter, audiovisual language sometimes tells viewers how to interpret what they are hearing and seeing. No language communicates perfectly or eliminates variations of interpretation. One recent movie that probably would have passed unnoticed if it hadn't become controversial was condemned by one Catholic group as anti-Catholic, described by a conservative Catholic magazine as not anti-Catholic but liberal Catholic, and considered by the filmmaker himself (an active Catholic) as a satirical exploration of serious issues. Similar contrasting perceptions swirled around the short-lived TV series *Nothing Sacred*, which attracted a lot of controversy but not much of an audience. Condemned as anti-Catholic by some, the drama about an inner-city Catholic parish and its offbeat pastoral team was created by a Jesuit priest living in an inner-city Catholic parish. More recently, a student in my college class wrote a paper criticizing what she considered the antireligious slant of TV's *The Simpsons*. Not long after, the Evangelical Protestant magazine *Christianity Today* lauded the satirical cartoon's sympathetic treatment of the Simpson family's Evangelical neighbor, Ned Flanders. Now there is a book on *The Gospel According to the Simpsons: The Spiritual Life of the World's Most Animated Family* by Mark I. Pinsky.

We saw earlier that creators of media embed in their productions the values that reflect their "first principles" and who they are. On the other end, consumers read those productions in the light of their own first principles and personal circumstances. Factors they bring with them to the understanding of media include some attributes they were born with and others they have picked up along the way, such as:

- race
- gender
- class
- family
- faith
- knowledge
- life experience
- frame of mind (or mood)
- preconceptions about the movie/show/song/game

In other words, we see things not as they are but as we are. That is why different audiences receive the same creative work differently. What seems humorous to one person may be viciously sexist to another. What one person sees as a tribute to a particular ethnic group may be denounced by another as a hurtful stereotype. The great actor Marlon Brando refused to accept an Academy Award

as Best Actor because of Hollywood's negative and stereotyped portrayals of native Americans, and yet the film for
which he was to be honored—*The Godfather*—reinforced
and even recreated stereotypes of Italian Americans.

The Power of the Audience

This principle of media literacy is the flip side of all
the others because it is about consumption instead of production. It says that the audience has power beyond pur-
chasing power—the power to make meaning. Yet it is a
power that few of us realize because it is one that we exercise unconsciously.

Active viewing and listening of media, the goal of the
media literacy movement, puts us as audience in control.
Media construct reality, but we can deconstruct media reality; media have commercial purposes, but we don't have
to buy into them; media embed the values of their creators,
but we can hold them up against our own values that come
to us from the gospel; media use unique languages, but
we can learn those languages both for enjoyment and as a
defense against their manipulation of our emotions. We can
even push the "off" button.

All of the suggestions in this book so far and all of
those to follow are directed toward making a more active
and aware media consumer, reading media with the eyes
of faith. Here are some ways to make your family more
aware of how different audiences receive the same message differently:

Never forget that your children do not have the same
depth of life experiences that you have to help them put
media into context. Unless someone tells them, they do not
realize that hitting someone with a chair repeatedly could
put that person in the hospital for days—or that it is wrong
to do so. A Saturday morning cartoon will not tell them
that; you have to.

When your children want to watch or play something
that you think is inappropriate, talk with them. Find out

how they are perceiving it; tell them how you are. You may be getting very different messages. Instead of overreacting when you find out they have seen something you wish they had not, use this as an opportunity to help them analyze and evaluate what they have seen. In the course of the conversation, convey your values.

With something that you particularly like or particularly dislike, ask how someone else might view it—such as a member of a group depicted, your parents or children, your greatest hero or Jesus.

Pick a particular character. How would you like this portrayal if you were a member of that character's race, ethnic group, age group, or profession? Then ask people you know in some of those categories if they saw the show or movie and what they thought it was saying about them.

Family Dialogue Questions

- *Which of your favorite shows or games are controversial? Why? Do you think critics miss the point or misunderstand the message?*

- *When have you ever disagreed with someone about what a movie or TV show means? Which of you was right?*

- *What shows or movies have offended you? Why did you find them offensive? What do others say?*

Seven

X

Thank You, Thomas Edison

Thomas Edison, not the only father of the cinema but the one inventor best known to Americans, started something big. It killed vaudeville and refused to be killed by television.

Cinema is the art form of the masses. Movies reflect the tastes, myths and worries of the age, the views and values of the people who pay to see them, says noted media educator David Considine of Appalachian State University. That means they provide a window on the culture—especially the culture of youth. For children and adolescents now see more movies, and see the same movie more often, than their parents.

Films can also deliver great drama and great comedy in permanent form. A few films, like *Life Is Beautiful*, even do both. No one living today has ever seen the great nineteenth century actor Edwin Booth, but a century from now our descendants will be able to see Laurence Olivier in his prime. With VCRs and DVDs, there is really no such thing as an old movie.

Even more important, movies can deal "with themes of great meaning and value from an ethical and spiritual point of view," as Pope John Paul II wrote in his 1995 World Communications Day message, "Of Films and Human Values."

The Trouble with Movies

But, as we have seen in previous chapters and know from our own viewing experience, movies—like other mass media—often condone sex outside of marriage, lack positive values (honesty and integrity, fidelity, kindness, tolerance, decency, trust), portray violence as the only solution to problems, value persons by what they own and how they look, ignore the religious community and stereotype people by ages, genders and ethnic groups.

Other problems with films include:

Misrepresentation of history that may be mistaken as fact. Disney's *Pocahontas* is one example, as are presentations of dubious theories of history, such as Oliver Stone's *JFK* and *Nixon*.

Heavy use of alcohol, tobacco and illegal drugs. Two federal agencies surveyed two hundred popular movies from 1996 and 1997 and found that ninety-eight percent contained smoking, drinking or drug use.

The symbiotic relationship between toy makers and Hollywood, producing what has been called "entertoyment." Toy makers rely on licensed characters for nearly half of their total retail sales each year. That means that many movies rated G for acceptability to children could be rated C for commercialism. What is wrong with that? This is: Movie-related toys that give kids prepackaged characters and well-defined roles may limit their imaginations, at least in the opinion of some psychologists.

These latter concerns are relatively new, but the church was worried about the moral content of films even during what we now regard as the Golden Age of Hollywood. The Catholic bishops of the United States founded the National Legion of Decency in 1934, five years before Clark Gable so famously uttered the first "damn" in a motion picture. At a time when even married couples slept in twin beds in films, faithful Catholics would stand in church once a year and pledge to see only decent movies.

The U.S. bishops have somewhat revived that approach through their five-year "Renewing the Mind of the Media Campaign," which goes beyond just movies. Parishioners in participating dioceses are asked in church to sign a card pledging in part "to encourage in all forms of media whatever upholds moral values, strengthens families, and promotes a just and peaceful society" and "reject media that produce immoral content and demean the dignity of the human person." Many media literacy advocates have roundly criticized the effort as too negative in its approach.

Art in Celluloid

There is more to films than just moral content, important as that is. There is also artistic content, the true and the beautiful. If our only criterion in picking films is to avoid the negative and even the harmful, then we put the most laughless comedy and the most powerful drama in the same category as long as they both avoid sex, violence and profanity.

We can do better.

As discerning filmgoers, we should pay attention both to artistic merit and to moral content. One of the strengths of the movie reviews from the U.S. bishops' Office for Film and Broadcasting, cited in chapter four, is that they consider both—and that they recognize the difference. Not every decent movie is a good movie. The complete description of the Office's "A-I General Patronage" category, for example, notes that the film contains nothing morally objectionable but "does not mean the movie is recommended, or is free of fleeting scary moments for young children."

Sometimes art can be challenging. The church makes room for that. When the Vatican compiled a list of forty-five films of artistic and religious merit to celebrate the hundredth anniversary of film in 1995, the list included three movies that had been rated B for morally objectionable by the Legion of Decency when they were new. Today the Office for Film and Broadcasting would not give those movies—*Open City* (1945), *The Bicycle Thief* (1949) and *La Strada* (1954)—an equivalent rating. What has changed is that the church today looks at the film as a whole rather than an individual scene that may be objectionable. The Office of Film and Broadcasting has a category called "A-IV Adults, with Reservations" for movies that require some caution and are not for casual entertainment. "Though not morally offensive in itself," the description notes, "the film may require some analysis and interpretation to avoid false conclusions."

Age-Appropriate

Adults can make those analyses and interpretations, using the principles of media literacy outlined in this book and the principles of the gospel. However, as the bishops' rating system recognizes, some movies are not for kids, even kids who are armed with the proper interpretive filters and parents to help them. "Given the power of film, what might be a tasteful and realistic portrayal of a significant human experience for a disciplined and mature adult can result, for sensitive and vulnerable young people, in self-destructive, antisocial behavior," Cardinal Roger Mahony writes in his wonderful pastoral letter "Film Makers, Film Viewers: Their Challenges and Opportunities"(http://carcardinal.la-archdiocese.org/920915.html).

"The industry's NC-17 rating is of limited help, since most of our young people reach emotional maturity much later than seventeen years of age."

Whereas an R rating—at least in theory—means that a person under seventeen won't be admitted without an accompanying parent or adult, NC-17 (which was called "X" before 1990) is supposed to mean that no one under seventeen is admitted at all. The Cardinal rightly disputes the notion that maturity suddenly arrives at age seventeen. As we noted in chapter one, only parents who know their children can really decide what is "age-appropriate" for them, although ratings and reviews may help.

Enjoying the Movies

Parents face a complex challenge in helping their kids find movies that are high quality, high morality—and high interest for young people. The task is all the tougher because Hollywood does not do much to promote movies without lucrative licensing deals attached. Consider "The Hyped and the Hypeless: Fate of Two Films." That's what *The Wall Street Journal* called its 1995 story about the films *Congo*, a huge box-office hit generally lambasted by critics, and *A Little Princess*, a box-office dud that most critics hailed as one of the best films of the year. What happened? *Congo* had special effects and big merchandising tie-ins. Warner Brothers, apparently embarrassed, later reissued *A Little Princess* with more fanfare.

In addition to general suggestions in earlier chapters applying to all media, which may be worth reviewing now, here are some ideas for finding good movies—including challenging ones—for all members of the family:

Make movies special from the time your kids are small. Pick a night to be your family video night, with popcorn and other treats. Or go out to movies as a family (especially for those films that play better on a big screen, such as space epics). Either approach is well suited to grandparents as well as parents. Afterward, talk about the movie. Use some of the questions about reality, commercialism, values and languages from earlier chapters.

Enjoy the classics. When I was a kid I could only see the great Disney movies on *The Wonderful World of Disney* once a week and *Citizen Kane* or *Casablanca* on late-night TV cut up with lots of commercials. DVDs and VCRs make it possible to enjoy the best of the filmmaker's art any time. I have a goddaughter who grew up as familiar with the good old stuff as with the latest releases. Her family dared to watch black and white movies! Several lists of worthwhile films appear in the "Resources" chapter at the end of this book. Another way to find the classics is to check out the "Family Video of the Week" from the U.S. bishops' Office for Film and Broadcasting on-line at

www.uscccb.org/movies/index.htm or on the telephone at
1–800–311–4CCC. (Some of these great old films may
embody stereotypical or even negative portrayals of ethnic groups. Confront this issue as it arises. Talk about it as
a reflection of the culture of the time.)

Do not overlook your parish and diocesan resources.
If your parish or diocese has a media center that includes
videos, make that one of your first places to look for quality films that reflect gospel values.

Avoid movies that are essentially feature-length commercials for a line of toys.

Get videos—and advice—from your public library.
Although you cannot guarantee that all the librarians share
your value system, they can usually steer you to the better movies appropriate for your family.

Take out only one video at a time. Let the experience
soak in instead of following it immediately with another
movie. Keep a list of movies you want to see, and use it
on your next trip to the library or video store.

When you find a good movie, buy it and add it to your
video library. Like a good book, it is worth watching more
than once and you will see new things in it each time that
will help you enjoy it at a new level.

Take turns picking the movie. If kids choose a less-
than-classic movie occasionally, that is no disaster. You will
have your chance to express that opinion when you talk
about it afterward. Besides, you get to pick, too.

Older kids go to lots of movies with other kids to social-
ize. Obviously, they are not going to invite you along!
Nevertheless, you can still be part of the experience.
Suggest movies to them that you have seen and enjoyed.
(Be careful not to force movies on them with a "this is good
for you approach," like unpleasant medicine.) Ask their
opinions about a movie they have seen. Without interro-
gating, ask how they liked it and why. See the movie yourself and then discuss it again. Express your own values.
Have the same kind of discussion you would have if you
saw the film together.

If you have a video camera, help younger kids make their own movies. This is a great way for them to experience how filmmakers create reality, using special languages and incorporating their own viewpoints. And the finished product can be a great way to keep grandparents up to date on what they are doing. Maybe this home production can be the basis of a Family Movie Night.

Family Dialogue Questions

- *What is your favorite movie? Why? What makes it better than your next-favorite movie? How often do you get a new favorite movie?*

- *What is the difference between seeing a movie in a theater and watching it on a VCR or DVD player? How does watching on a large screen in a dark room with a sound system help you get into the screen reality compared with watching at home? Which do you prefer?*

- *For younger kids: How do you play with toys based on a movie? Do you act out the movie or do you create your own movie?*

Eight

✗

The Circus of the Screen

In the satirical film *Network*, a TV anchorman known as "the Mad Prophet of the Airwaves" reminds his audience that television is not the truth: "Television is a circus, a carnival, a traveling troupe of acrobats, story tellers, dancers, singers, jugglers, side show freaks, lion tamers and football players."

More than a quarter of a century later, TV is still all of that and more. It is the greatest twenty-four-hours-a-day entertainment and information machine ever invented. Only the computer comes close, thanks to the Internet. But the Internet still does not have the almost-universal reach of television. TV is the predominate shaper of images and teller of tales in our culture today, strongly supported by all the other mass media that feed off of it and play into it. And as George Gerbner, dean emeritus of the Annenberg School for Communication at the University of Pennsylvania once said, "If you can write a nation's stories, you needn't worry about who makes its laws."

Television tells America's stories—not parents, not the church. By the age of sixty-five the average American will have spent thirteen years in front of a television compared to four and a half months in church. To pluralize the understatement of TV-raised Chance Gardener in the book and film *Being There*, "We like to watch." It starts early. By one estimate, American kids are watching TV an average of six hours a week at one year old, an age at which the American

Association of Pediatrics says they shouldn't be watching at all. Older children watch more than three hours a day. By the time they reach eighteen, kids have spent more hours in front of a television set than they have in front of a blackboard.

And they are not just watching "children's TV." In one Catholic school, fourth and fifth graders told teachers their favorite show was the animated *South Park*, broadcast at 10 p.m. on the Comedy Central channel with a TV–MA rating (mature audiences only, unsuitable for children under seventeen). Many parents might think that children ten to twelve years old should be in bed at that hour, not watching adult fare. But a reasonable bedtime is no guarantee that children will not watch programs meant for their parents. The 3 to 8 p.m. time slots, prime viewing periods for kids, are loaded with syndicated reruns of programs rated TV–14 (parents strongly cautioned, unsuitable for children under fourteen). Then at 8 p.m., at one time the beginning of the "family hour" when networks voluntarily offered family-friendly programming, children can watch first-run sex and violence. As a *Wall Street Journal* headline once reported, "It's 8 p.m. Your Kids Are Watching Sex on TV." If you are not with them, odds are good that that is just what they are doing.

And it is getting worse. A Parents Television Council analysis of two hundred hours of programming aired during the family hour in the 2000–2001 season found the sex rawer than the previous season—and the language cruder. TV viewers today hear a lot of trash talk that used to be rare even in theatrical films. Four-letter words can be a cheap substitute for creativity when writers use their shock value to get an easy laugh or demonstrate a character's mood. Cable started it and the broadcast networks joined in to keep from losing audience share.

The legal requirement that television stations provide three hours of educational programming for children per week, and all the noble efforts to improve TV for children, have no impact on children actually watching the tube. As communications professor Joshua Meyrowitz says in his book *No Sense of Place*, "There is no children's television." Children mostly watch the same programs that adults watch, not the ones labeled for children.

What do they learn there? As we have seen in earlier chapters, television's stories tell us that:

- What is on TV is what is real and what is important.
- America is violent, sexy, non-religious, predominantly male, overwhelmingly white and young, with most characters presented as stereotypes.
- Things—products we can buy—will make us who we want to be.
- Sex without responsibility or consequence, violence against evil, instant gratification, wealth, success and physical perfection (defined by supermodels) are good.

These are all good reasons for improving your Quantity/Quality Quotient. But content is not the only problem with television. TV affects us in negative ways that have nothing to do with what's on the screen, and that argues for cutting the time spent with the tube (quantity) regardless of content (quality).

Beyond Content

Television can pull families apart in a number of different ways. The most obvious way is physically. Where TV in earlier decades was known as "the electronic hearth" that the family gathered around in the living room or family room, most families now have multiple TV sets that they watch separately. More than half of children (and sixty-five percent of those eight or older) now have a TV in their bedroom, according to the Kaiser Foundation's "Kids and Media at the New Millennium" report and other studies.

TV can distance family members from each other emotionally as well—parents from children and from each other. This problem is not only for families including children. Empty nesters and childless couples also face the danger of watching TV and videos or DVDs as their primary "couple" activity, one that does little to foster intimacy and relationship unless they work at sharing their reactions with each other. But the unreflective use of media can be particularly harmful for children. Organizers of the fifth International TV Turnoff Week in 1999 published a poem that captured the sense of this: "Lord, turn me into a television. So that my parents will care for me the way they do the television. So that Mommy will look at me with the same interest she looks at the soap operas, and Daddy will look at me the way he does the ball games. Lord, please, let me be a television, even if only for a day."

Parents frequently set their children in front of a set and tell them to be quiet. Then they may be surprised if their children ignore them when they walk into a room. Case in point: A family who visited an acquaintance of mine in his home for just a couple of hours brought along a VCR, a monitor, and videotapes. The parents hooked up the electronics in a bedroom to keep the kids amused while the adults socialized. This is TV as babysitter, TV as electronic tranquillizer. And some parents even take it on the road: A popular option for minivans and SUVs is an entertainment center with TV, VCR, video game and headphones that let kids and adults (but fortunately not the driver) listen to separate music.

The American Academy of Pediatrics said in 1999 that healthy brain development in young children requires direct interaction with parents and other caregivers. The Academy warned that children under the age of two should not be left to be raised by Barney and the Teletubbies. It urged no TV at all until age two, and no more than two hours a day for children between the ages of two and five. TV cuts deeply into playtime, as well as affecting the imaginative content of play by presenting kids with prepackaged stories to act out.

When TV does not lead people to ignore each other, it can cause them to battle each other. Fights over the remote control have become a familiar domestic scene and the frequent subject of comic strips. In one such, for example, the Born Loser's wife complains: "Don't I ever get a say in this house? Shouldn't my voice be heard? Isn't it about time I be treated as an equal when it comes to making decisions around here?" In the last panel we get a broader view of the couple so that we can now see they are sitting in front of a television set. "Oh, all right," the husband concedes. "You can have the remote!" Is the wife angry at this obvious condescension? By no means: she has a broad smile on her face.

The remote control itself, now almost as universal as television, has a number of disturbing side effects. The device:

- Teaches us to expect immediate satisfaction of our desires. It should be no surprise that a Garfield cartoon has the lasagna-loving cat staring out the window with a remote control in his hand thinking "Change! Darn you!" A sales brochure for a particular brand of remote control, one that is shaped like a gun and comes with sound effects to match, promises "instant gratification and stress relief."

- Encourages the desire for constant stimulation by making it so easy to look for something more stimulating whenever we get bored. One result may be that TV producers create ever more sensationalistic programming to hold viewers and not lose them to other stations.

- Bombards the viewer with disassociated images that teach lack of connection. Story and linear thought are lost.

The Virtues of Television

It is tempting to be so overwhelmed by the negative aspects of television—both its content and its sociological effects—that we want to trash the tube. Some individuals and families have done so, many of them for religious reasons, with few regrets. "So much inimical to a life of faith is on TV," Carol Begley, an active Catholic who home-schools her four-year-old and ten-year-old sons, told the Associated Press. "I think it's easier for a child to learn to pray and have a spiritual life if he's not living a life of electronic distractions." Dr. Begley, a classics scholar, and her husband, also a Ph.D., decided not to have a television in their home in Georgia, Vermont. That is a valid lifestyle option. However, I disagree with one Arlington, Virginia, father who said, "TV is just an unavoidable evil." In the hands of careful consumers, TV can be much more. It has the power to:

Enrich family life. That is what Pope John Paul II said in his 1994 World Communications Day message on "Television and the Family." He went on to say that TV "can draw family members closer together and foster their solidarity with other families and with the community at large." Instead of pulling the family apart, TV can still be "the electronic hearth" for families who choose to watch television and videos together. "We do enjoy watching some of the new family programming (*Seventh Heaven, The Gilmore Girls*) together and often find it sparks good conversations with the kids," said Christie Brown, a Cincinnati area accountant and mother of two children, ages twelve and fourteen.

Bring people together around the country and the world. As the pope hinted, TV also unites our nation around big events like a presidential impeachment or a disputed presidential election. And it provides a shared experience and a common language as strangers jokingly accuse one another of being the weakest link or ask each other "Is that your final answer?" Rich and poor, illiterates and Ph.D.'s join in. They probably watch the same shows. Even if they do not, they know about them anyway.

Educate. It is almost a cliché that all television is educational television. TV always teaches. But here I mean the good things that TV teaches. the Public Broadcasting System, the Discovery Channel, the History Channel and even well done programs from the major networks occasionally live up to the original promise of TV as a great education machine.

Entertain and inform. TV's entertainment all too often appeals to the lowest common denominator, and its informational content is heavily laden with celebrity gossip. But TV at its best can do both of these well, making quality entertainment and information available even to people who cannot afford a movie or read a newspaper. Newton Minow, the Federal Communications Commission Chairman who famously dubbed TV "a vast wasteland" in 1961, said forty years later that he does not affirm admirers who tell him they do not have televisions. "I say, 'Well, you are missing life. You are closing the door to what's going on in the world,'" Minow told the Reuters news service. "I think television is very important."

Inspire. In both its fiction and nonfiction genres, TV has the capacity to tell stories of faith, hope, love, courage, fidelity, thanksgiving, reconciliation and other great theological themes. Such stories hold the transformative power to make us better people and better Christians. We saw in chapter one how to find them.

Using TV Well

The key to keeping the Quantity/Quality Quotient in balance, of course, is to watch the right programs in the right way. All of the guidelines in chapter one apply to television, plus the following as well:

Kick the TV *habit.* Do not turn on the tube as soon as you enter a room—but do turn it off as soon as you leave. "The most important thing to notice about television is that its natural position is off," British Broadcasting

Corporation producer Iwan Russell-Jones once told me. The first question should not be *what* to watch, but *whether* to watch. And that should be based on what is on. You are watching programs, not just television. Do not channel surf. "Be selective and plan ahead," wrote James E. and Lynette J. Smith of Washington, D.C., who have five of their own children and are raising three others. Use a TV schedule. Check the plot outlines to find shows that look promising. Require your children to tell you why they want to watch a show before you allow them to do so. (Entertainment is an acceptable reason once they learn to realize that entertainment is not value-free.)

Look for the EI designation in TV listings for children's shows, meaning they are educational/informational. Federal law requires broadcast stations to air three hours of such programming per week. You may want to make some of this part of your media diet, along with comedies, dramas, sports and other genres.

Think and pray hard about whether you want cable TV in your home. More access to programming means more reasons to watch TV (although there's always the complaint of the Bruce Springsteen song, "fifty-seven channels and nothin' on"). If you are not going to watch it, why pay for it? Another problem: It is hard to plan viewing ahead and avoid channel surfing with so many channels to surf. Our family has never subscribed to cable. I have found that cable's best educational and entertainment programs, particularly from Arts and Entertainment, are available on video at our public library. But many families that make an active effort to manage media keep cable for the family-oriented channels and round-the-clock news, while blocking out those channels that are questionable. To cable or not to cable is an important decision that you have to make based on what will best help your family keep its Quantity/Quality Quotient in line.

If you decide to keep or get cable service, consider subscribing to *Cable in the Classroom* magazine (www.cicon-line.org). It is a guide to more than five hundred hours of educational and family entertainment programming each month, sorted out by topic (English/Language Arts, History, Mathematics, etc.). It also has educational articles. Homeschoolers might find the publication particularly helpful, despite its clear purpose of promoting the cable channels. You can get a free copy by calling 1–800–216–2225.

Do not encourage small children to watch television before they are even interested. (I plead guilty to this one!) Remember, the American Academy of Pediatrics recommends no TV or videos at all for children under the age of two.

Resist the temptation to use TV as a babysitter. This is hard because little ones get in the way, and TV is an easy way to get them out of the way. "When I come home from a ten-and-a-half hour day as a middle school teacher, the only way I can occupy my daughter while I make a meal is to have her watch a show on TV (PBS or Nick Jr.) or a video ("Barney" or "Blue's Clues,")" said an Orlando area mother of a two-year-old. "If not, I would bring home a lot of fast food meals." Some parents who pay careful attention to how much and what their children watch have told me they see nothing wrong with using TV as a babysitter of last resort in small doses—usually when they need to cook or take a shower and no one else is around to watch a preschooler. That is understandable. As the stay-at-home mother of a six-year-old daughter and two-year-old son, Stephanie Moore has the time available to take a different approach: "Involve them (children) in your day-to-day activities. Save the floor washing and sewing for times they are with a grandparent or asleep. I love to cook and bake and shared it with Julieanne. She knew how to crack eggs at age four!"

As much as possible, watch TV together as a family. Put the television set (only one, as recommended in chapter one) in a central location where everyone can watch it. "Sit in the room while they watch TV—even if you see that cartoon the fourth time," urged registered nurse Mary

Snow of Cincinnati, mother of an eight-year-old and an eleven-year old. That is the ideal.

Make sure the same room with your television also has books, magazines, board games and crafts. This is a family activity room, not a TV room.

Put the TV in a cabinet so it is not on view all the time. "Out of sight, out of mind works like a charm!" Mrs. Moore reported. Her computer is in the basement and her TV is in an armoire. When our children were small, we put the TV out of sight the wrong way—by relegating it to the basement family room. We thought it would make TV less accessible. It did—for us! As a result, we were often absent when children were watching because we had meals to make or chores to carry out elsewhere in the house.

Hunt for quality, and do not expect to find it only on public television and the more educational cable channels. The best of commercial television (*The West Wing, Law & Order* for adults) are as good as or better than you will find on your local PBS affiliate. And the silliest comedies served up on public TV (*Are You Being Served?* springs to mind) are as banal as anything on commercial TV. Check out new programs that look promising. *TV Guide* publishes a children's television issue each fall that looks at new programs and videos. The Family Friendly Programming Forum, made up of forty-eight major advertisers, has put up seed money to promote the development of family-friendly scripts. The Forum also sponsors the Family Television Awards each year to honor quality family shows.

As you choose programs together with your children, make it clear to them what your criteria are. Escapism is a perfectly valid reason for watching a sitcom; crude humor that debases the human person is an even better reason for *not* watching a sitcom.

Talk about each program and its values—before (if you know enough about it), during and after in ways that were discussed in chapter four. Do not let little stuff slide—such as the use of words like "stupid," "shut up" and "idiot" that one parent reported hearing on *Rugrats*. If you cannot watch together because of some adult business that has to be done while the kids are awake, consider letting them watch a favorite tape that you already have watched together. Never let younger children watch a TV show unless you have at least seen other episodes in the series and consulted a TV schedule for the plot outline of this episode. Talk with them about the show even if you did not get a chance to watch it with them.

Share and discuss with the family your favorite programs from when you were a kid, either by watching cable (where all TV shows live forever) or by renting a video. Talk about why you liked it and get the reactions of other family members. Discuss how it is different from first-run shows on TV now.

Do not watch TV during meals as surveys show that most people do, thus expanding the waistlines of America. (Overweight kids in a Baylor College of Medicine survey, for example, ate half of their meals in front of television. Other studies have linked obesity and television-watching, which is a sedentary activity often accompanied by snacking and watching commercials for sugary and fatty foods.) Use meals as family dialogue time, sharing your experiences of the day and your thoughts. It may be the only "down" time you spend together as a family.

Opt out of Saturday morning TV. "This is the time slot in which children are first hooked on the niche culture, youth fads and the idea that it is good for them to purchase their own identities at the mall," syndicated religion columnist Terry Mattingly wrote in the Orthodox Christian magazine *Again*. "Saturday morning TV is a parent-free zone."

Use the VCR to "time shift": Tape programs that are on at inconvenient times (such as while kids are doing homework) and watch later. Then zap through the commercials—except when you decide to pay special attention to what values they are selling along with products, and what techniques they are using to do so. Also, tape and play later programs that may be age-appropriate for some members of the family but not others.

Establish a family rule that it is OK to talk to a family member who is watching television. Moreover, if that person does not respond, the set should go off. Although many people may feel that TV is a member of the family, perhaps even the most interesting member, it is not a human being. A person is more important than any television program. For that reason, you should also make it a family rule to turn off the television when a guest enters the home.

Let TV be a starting point to learn more. Have a globe or atlas in the family activity room to discuss the town or country where a show is set or a sports team is based. Read more about the history, science, and the geography behind the story. Visit a museum, zoo or aquarium to see in real life something you have seen on the screen.

Family Dialogue Questions

- *What is your favorite TV show? What makes it better than your next favorite?*

- *Do you watch programs or do you just watch television? Can you remember the plot of the last show you watched?*

- *How would your life be different if TV had not been invented? How would the life of your family be different?*

Nine

✗

Cyberspace Cadets

I do not remember life without television. My children, who are all grown, do not remember life without the personal computer. Their children will never know life without cyberspace, especially E-mail and the World Wide Web.

We are just beginning to see the potential of cyberspace. We cannot yet fully know where it is going. But we do know that it's gaining popularity at a geometric rate, threatening to supplant television as the world champion entertainment/information source and eventually assimilate it as computer monitor and TV become one. The Internet delivers news and information faster than all but the cable news networks, and it is interactive. People shop, work and play on-line. And E-mail has become the way many families and friends communicate on a daily basis, whether they live on the other side of the planet from each other or on the other side of the house.

More than half of adults and three-quarters of students over the age of twelve ("screenagers") have access to the Internet, according to the Pew Internet and American Life Project—numbers that will have jumped still higher by the time you read this. Worldwide, as many as 380 million people may surf the Internet, visiting thirty million Web sites. A gender gap that once existed in Internet use has disappeared, with more women than men now on the Internet, and the racial gap is narrowing. The only remaining digital divide is an economic one, and even that is diminishing. Middle-income people are increasingly drawn to the Internet, and significant percentages of Internet users say they spend less time with TV, videos and radio. Even the poor have free on-line access at many of the nation's public libraries.

Some people unreflectively welcome the Internet as an alternative to television, especially parents who would prefer their kids spend time in cyberspace than on Planet TV. But cyberspace comes complete with some of the same negatives of other electronic media, and a few uniquely its own. It is vaster than the "vast wasteland" of television, but parts of it are also more wasted.

The Trouble with Cyberspace

The most harrowing aspect for any parent is that the Internet not only makes pornography available in the home—some of it legally, by virtue of a 1997 U.S. Supreme Court ruling—but can actually be a vehicle for pedophiles lurking in chat rooms to lure children into sexual encounters. Almost one out of five children who regularly go on-line have received sexual come-ons in cyberspace, according to a study conducted by the University of New Hampshire's Crimes Against Children Research Center and published in the *Journal of the American Medical Association* in 2001. Children are not the only ones in danger. Spouses cheating through "cybersex" have disrupted marriages.

But there are other troubling dimensions as well, relating to the essential nature, or form, of the Internet and what that means for the content.

For starters, there are no "gatekeepers" on the Internet, as there are with books, newspapers, and television. The whole point of the Internet is that it does not exist in any one place, and is under no central authority. It is the Wild West, with each Webmaster doing his or her own thing and no one to sort out the mass of information available. There is no one to separate the true from the false, the mainstream from the marginal, the good from the bad, and the important from the trivial.

Almost anyone can create a Web page—and almost anyone does. That is a mixed blessing. The web enables people of ordinary means and talents to publish their ideas, but is open to all kinds of perversions in the process. Several Catholic dioceses in the United States were hugely embarrassed when their old Web site addresses were taken over by pornography rings offering on-line smut. In addition to pornographers, hate groups and religious cults find a home in cyberspace—often with slick presentations that give them credibility with the naive, including children. I know a seventh-grade teacher who was not thrilled with a student who submitted a paper nonchalantly quoting a Web site reference to "dumb broads." Typing in *Harry Potter* in a search engine will yield thousands of Web sites, some of which deal with actual witchcraft rather than the delightful series of children's books. Religious sites using the label "Catholic" may actually oppose the teachings of the church.

At the same time, the content of the Internet is heavily commercial, with promotional material often disguised. *The Wall Street Journal* highlighted this in a "Personal Technology" column headlined: "Old-Fashioned Ethic of Separating Ads Is Lost in Cyberspace." Web sites for movies, to cite just one example, often are multimedia-advertising vehicles with 3-D graphics, film clips and interactive games.

Children are a major target of cybermarketing. Web sites for kids routinely glean marketing information under the guise of asking questions for a contest or a club. The Children's On-line Privacy Protection Act of 2000 requires Web sites to obtain "verifiable parental consent" before collecting, using or disclosing the name, address, or other information of children under thirteen. It mandates that Web sites geared to children have prominent links to the site's privacy policy. But a year after the law was passed, the University of Pennsylvania's Annenberg Public Policy Center checked 162 sites and found almost half were not in compliance. The sites examined included those for video games, snacks, children's characters and TV shows.

The Web is just one way in which cyberspace constructs reality. E-mail and chat rooms provide several others:

- Chat rooms built around a common interest of participants can foster one narrow view of the world, silencing opposing opinions with slamming.
- Gender and biography can be totally fabricated by a chat room participant and no one the wiser—a favorite technique of sexual predators. A famous New Yorker cartoon shows a dog typing on a computer and explaining to a canine friend, "On the Internet, nobody knows you're a dog."
- The lack of body language and facial expressions in E-mail, only partially remedied by the overly cute written code that has emerged as a substitute, sometimes leads to miscommunication.
- Urban legends, myths and rumors spread like prairie fire via E-mail, apparently faster than by word of mouth, and all kinds of junk information is taken seriously. You may have thought the one about Microsoft buying the Vatican was an obvious joke, but some people believed it.

At the other end of the computer, copying and pasting from the Internet makes plagiarism a two-click operation that is becoming increasingly common from grade school to graduate school. A young high school teacher in rural Kansas resigned in 2002 when the school board ordered her to give partial credit instead of zeroes to twenty-eight sophomore biology students who plagiarized their semester projects from the Internet.

What happens to human relations in the age of cyberspace? That may depend on who you are and how you use the Internet. Early studies by Stanford University's Institute for the Quantitative Study of Society and the Carnegie Mellon University Human-Computer Interaction Institute indicated that frequent cyberspace visitors are isolated from others, even sad and lonely. However, other academic work has found just the opposite, at least for some people. Geriatric expert David Lansdale of Stanford contends that E-mail and other Internet uses help overcome four plagues of institutionalized elders: loneliness, boredom, helplessness and decline of mental skills. And the Pew Internet & American Life Project found that the Internet, particularly E-mail, enhances social interaction.

A follow-up study by the Carnegie Mellon researchers, reported in 2001, may explain the differences in other surveys. It found that extroverts tend to feel better about themselves when they use the Internet, probably because they use it for social interaction. But introverts, using the Internet most often for solo activities such as games, tend to feel lonelier after spending a lot of time in cyberspace. When the first Carnegie Mellon study began in 1995, not many people used it for interacting with others because less than twenty percent of the population had Internet access at the time. Therefore, that study highlighted the negative effects of cyberspace. Without exaggerating that potential, it is safe to say that too much time on-line can be harmful for some people.

Certainly the downside of cyberspace is there on the margins. A small percentage of Internet users, perhaps many with underlying mental problems to begin with, are so addicted to the Internet that they cannot control the hours they spend there. They even neglect loved ones and responsibilities, just as other addicts do. Dr. Nathan Andrew Shapiro, while researching the phenomenon as a third year resident at the University of Cincinnati, called them "Internetomaniacs."

Safe and Sound in Cyberspace

However, for all of its troublesome aspects, cyberspace is one of the great blessings of the mass mediated age. The Internet affords its users access to a vast database of information twenty-four hours a day, saving incredible amounts of time. It makes it possible to work from home through a computer, a particular boon to those who are home-bound and those who choose to work at home to be with their children. E-mail and Web sites from resistance groups have been tremendous weapons against oppression around the world. Within the family, E-mail can connect those who are separated, while the computer itself can be a new electronic hearth for family members that live under the same roof.

I urge anyone who can afford it to acquire a computer and Internet access if they do not have them already. The following guidelines will help the whole family journey safely in cyberspace.

Having the computer in your family activity room, where you spend most of your time as a family, and including cyberspace in your media time limits will eliminate many concerns. Although you are not going to read E-mail over your child's shoulder—I hope!—you will be able to see any visually inappropriate material. Share the adventure of going on-line with your children often. Since you cannot be with your children every hour of their busy days and yours, some other guidelines are necessary.

"The starting point of safe Internet use is to recognize that the rules you live by in the real world apply in cyberspace, too," the Catholic bishops of the United States write in their excellent statement "Your Family and Cyberspace" (www.usccb.org/comm/cyberspace.htm). "If you tell your children not to talk to strangers, the same applies on the Internet. Just as you ordinarily expect your children to tell you where they are going, ask them with whom they log on when they 'go out' on the Internet. You listen to your children when they talk about their friends, so listen to them when they talk about what they're finding on the Internet."

Remember and remind your children that "On the Internet, nobody knows you're a dog." An E-mail correspondent that you have never met may not be as advertised. Never give out any sort of personal information on-line to someone you don't know, such as age, full address, financial status or data about your children.

Talk with your children about the potential dangers in cyberspace, while trying not to make them overly fearful. Drawing largely on the safety rules developed by the National Center for Missing and Exploited Children, caution them to never:

- fill out a questionnaire or give out any kind of personal information (name, address, telephone number, school) on-line, not even for a game or contest;
- send a photo or anything else on-line without checking with you first;
- respond to an E-mail that is belligerent, suggestive, or makes them uncomfortable in any way; instead they should notify you so you can contact the on-line service;
- do anything that hurts people or is against the law;
- give out their Internet passwords to anybody but you;
- buy anything on-line without parental permission;
- pretend to be someone they are not (older or a different sex, for example);
- agree to get together with anyone they have met on-line without checking with you first.

If you ever do permit your child to meet a cyberfriend in person, make it in a public place and go with your child.

Let younger children use your E-mail, not have their own. Elizabeth Starr, of Arlington, Virginia, follows that policy and others with her ten-year-old son. "He does not have a personal E-mail address, and does not know the password to get into the whole computer, only to his games and research aids for school work," she reported. "I don't allow my son to play games with unknown people of any age on the computer, or to have computer pen pals. He's not allowed to participate in chat rooms. He can use our E-mail system to write friends or relatives." With age comes privileges, of course, and opening of an E-mail address in an older child's name might be a rite of passage.

Encourage children to tell you if they see or read anything on-line that makes them uncomfortable, whether in an E-mail, a chat room or on a Web site. Do not overreact if they do—you do not want to discourage them from communicating with you. But if someone sends them child pornography (which is still illegal) or attempts to solicit them sexually, contact the Internet Service Provider and the FBI.

Set boundaries regarding on-line areas so your children know you care what they encounter in cyberspace. Kathy Olson, a pediatric speech therapist, and her husband, an accountant, only let their twelve-year-old son visit Web sites they've been to with him, and only send E-mail to people they know. "I periodically ask about screen names I see," Olson said. The son balks at the restrictions. "He is still naive about the safety," she said, "but I think he sees my passion about this."

As a backup, try to get Internet access through an Internet Service Provider that excludes at least some inappropriate material and has parental controls that let you restrict access to chat rooms, news groups and some Web sites. Or buy and use a stand-alone Internet filtering program even though they are imperfect, as noted in chapter four. Some popular brands include SurfWatch, Net Nanny, CyberSitter, and CyberPatrol.

Ideally, there should be a level of trust in the family that will leave you comfortable that your children will follow the boundaries about the kinds of sites they can visit. But if you have a reason to be concerned, check out your browser's "history" feature to see a listing of where they (and you) have been.

Make sure your child understands that all of the rules for safe Internet use apply not only at home but also on any computer they use, such as those at school, at the library or at a friend's house.

Do not assume that something is true because it is on the Internet, especially if it sounds strange or is counter to what you already know. What is the source of the Web site? What is the content? (Especially: Is this advertising in disguise? Does this sound reasonable or not in light of other things you know?) What is the source of the content? (An advertiser? A hate group?) What are the links—are they credible or suspect?

Ask these questions and more about any Web site using the Catholic label. As I point out in "The Church in Cyberspace," a brochure I wrote for the Archdiocese of Cincinnati, Web sites with "Catholic" in the name may actually be anti-Catholic propaganda sites. Or they may represent points of view held by some Catholics but not representative of the church universal. They may provide misinformation, or mix good information with bad theology.

If the generator of the Web site is an official arm of the church—the Vatican, a diocese, or a Catholic parish—then the site is certainly Catholic. But be careful. Using the name of a parish or (arch)diocese does not mean that the site is genuine. If you did not receive the Web address from a reliable source or if anything on it looks questionable, check it out with a call to the supposed source. Any site that is not what it seems to be should not be trusted on its content.

Not all good Catholic material on the web comes from church authorities, however. If the source is not official, is it reputable? Is it credible? Perhaps you do not know because you have never heard of the organization behind the site or because the organization is not identified. Then you should find out more about it. Consider the content. It may come from reliably Catholic sources, such as official teaching documents of the church, even if the operator of the site is not official or familiar. If the site does not have links to the U.S. Conference of Catholic Bishops (www. usccb.org) and the Vatican (www.vatican.va), that's reason to question how Catholic the site really is. For a brief listing of reliable Catholic Web sites, check out the "Resources" chapter. For a monthly look at what is new in on-line Catholicism, check out the Web Catholic column on www.AmericanCatholic.org.

Be on the lookout for good Web sites on other subjects,

too—those that entertain and those that inform. Share yours with friends and family and ask them for theirs.

Only use E-mail to communicate with your family—or with anyone, for that matter—when it is the best way available. In the hierarchy of communication, E-mail has the great advantage of immediacy in comparison to a traditional letter or card. It is easier to write and faster to send. But it is a supplement, not a substitute, for face-to-face contact whenever possible and the occasional phone call in between. I have friends in several states and four countries that our family e-mails regularly. It is a great way to stay in touch. But hearing their voices is better, and being with them is best of all.

Let cyberspace bring members of your family together. Encourage older kids to create a family Web site, being careful not to reveal too many specifics. Do not feel self-conscious if your children know more than you do in this area; let them teach you. If grandparents live in another city, have grandchildren e-mail them frequently. If they live in the same city, encourage grandchildren to go on-line with grandparents to show them how to access news and information about hobbies, sports and religion. If grandparents are reluctant to enter the digital culture, assure them that they have one or more personal consultants to get them started and keep them going—their grandchildren!

If you or any member of your family spend an exorbitant amount of time with on-line chatting, playing games, gambling or shopping to the neglect of important family and work responsibilities, and find yourself unable to stop, it may be time to seek professional help. You can get general information from the Center for On-line Addiction (www.netaddiction.com) and Computer Addiction Services (www.computeraddiction.com).

Finally, try to remember that not everything in the world responds to the click of a mouse—and neither does God. Allow time in your life for the things that take time: prayer and spiritual development, personal relationships, growth in understanding.

Family Dialogue Questions

- *Whom do you e-mail? Why do you use that form of communication? Have you spent time with them in person? Would you rather e-mail or talk with those people in person?*

- *What are your favorite World Wide Web sites? What do you like most about each? Is the interest more what it looks like or what it says?*

- *How do you know if what you read on a Web site is true? Have you ever seen anything on a Web site that you disbelieved?*

Ten

✗

Toward Optimum Q/Q

From the first chapter of this book, you have been learning why you should get your Q/Q (Quantity/Quality) Quotient in line, and how to do it. Have your media habits changed as a result? To find out, go back to chapter one and rework the media use chart.

If you do not see a difference, you have not been working at it. By now, you have a whole tool kit of techniques for managing mass media. And you know from the witness of other parents quoted in these pages that you can succeed if you are persistent and consistent about taking charge of all those screens in your family life.

Do not stop there.

Pass this book on to your spouse and to grandparents, godparents, babysitters, neighbors, teachers and members of your faith community.

Ask your school to incorporate media literacy into the curriculum. Or volunteer to present supplementary programs on the subject, as members of the St. Mary School Parent Media Awareness Group do for grades K–2 at their Cincinnati parish. (The group also sponsors an annual presentation for parents on some aspect of media.)

Get your parish to promote good media by starting or upgrading a parish media center and by presenting a film festival. The "Resources" chapter at the end of this book suggests some high quality films. Your (arch)diocesan media center can also help.

Ask your public and school libraries to purchase particular videos that you have found to be of high quality. Or even donate a copy.

Develop a list of non-violent toys as the Peace and Justice Commission of St. Clare Parish in Portland, Oregon, does each Christmas.

Write to local stations, networks and advertisers to criticize or, especially, praise worthwhile programs. Get your kids involved in writing, too. (The "Resources" chapter includes addresses of major broadcast networks.)

When you start talking with others about the problems and the promise of media in the family, you will quickly learn that you are not alone in your concerns. All spouses and parents face the same issues, and some have developed their own solutions. Become allies. Share information. Learn from each other. And pray:

God of Word and Sacrament,
give us the courage to be discerning consumers
of mass media,
critiquing and encouraging media productions
in our families and in the church.
Bless our efforts to find and support
productions that entertain, enlighten and inspire,
for they are truly gifts of the Spirit.
In Jesus' name we pray,
Amen.

RESOURCES

—————— ✗ ——————

Books

This is, obviously, only a tiny sampling of books available on media for families. It does not even include all the books I have quoted from or cited. Rather, I have chosen to list here only those books that I believe parents will find the most informative and practical.

Andriacco, Dan. *Screen Saved: Peril and Promise of Media in Ministry.* Cincinnati: St. Anthony Messenger Press, 2000. An exploration of how the characteristics of the mass media have affected cultural expectations of all our institutions, including the church, and how church ministers should respond. About half the chapters should be of interest to anyone involved in the church, and about one fourth should be enlightening to anyone who cares about how media affect our minds and our souls.

Axelrod, Lauryn. *TV-Proof Your Kids: A Parent's Guide to Safe and Healthy Viewing.* Secaucus, N.J.: Carol Publishing Co., 1997. An insightful approach to managing television from the viewpoint of a parent and experienced media literacy teacher. Her primary tool is what she calls TV Talk with kids, and she gives examples in each chapter. She also offers many questions to ask kids while watching TV to help them grapple with commercialism, violence, bias in the news and other concerns. In the final chapters, she goes beyond TV to discuss videos, the Internet and electronic games, with some tips on how kids can make their own videos.

DeGaetano, Gloria, and Bander, Kathleen. *Screen Smarts: A Family Guide to Media Literacy.* Boston: Houghton Mifflin Co., 1996. An analysis of the problems of violence, advertising, biased news and screen stereotypes, primarily in television and games. More than one hundred activities for adults to do with children make this an excellent resource for home schooling families.

Grossman, Lt. Col. Dave, and DeGaetano, Gloria. *Stop Teaching Our Kids to Kill: A Call to Action Against TV, Movie & Video Game Violence.* New York: Crown Publishers, 1999. The subtitle almost says it all. A strong review of the evidence linking media and violence, capped at the end by good lists of resources (organizations, where to write, chronology of major findings on media violence, etc.)

Murphy, Jane, and Tucker, Karen. *Stay Tuned! Raising Media-Savvy Kids in the Age of the Channel-Surfing Couch Potato.* New York: Doubleday, 1996. A lively guide for parents, nicely packaged with whimsical illustrations and sidebars. The authors, producers of videos for kids, emphasize using the VCR to gain control of television. Strengths of the book include information on child development and lists of "Things to Consider" and "What You Can Do" in dealing with various problem areas you might encounter in videos.

Postman, Neil, and Powers, Steve. *How to Watch TV News.* New York: Penguin Books, 1992. Postman, a social critic, and Powers, a television journalist, approach broadcast news with a critical eye that they pass on to the reader, along with the tools for perceptive analysis. They take the reader behind the scenes to examine the conventions of the TV newscast, its working requirements and its flaws. The central truth that television is a commercial enterprise, driven by the need to boost ratings in order to increase the value of commercial time, is never far from the authors' focus. Their chapter on "The Commercial" is a fine analysis of the commercial as religious parable.

Walsh, David, Ph.D. *Selling Out America's Children: How America Puts Profits Before Values and What Parents Can Do.* Minneapolis: Fairview Press, 1994. The author, a family psychologist, makes a strong case that the values most parents have for their children are not the values now supported by the broader society. He discusses how television and advertising, which view children purely as profit centers, promote consumerism, instant gratification, life without pain and constant stimulation in the form of media violence. Values lost in the process, he argues, include patience, moderation and self-discipline. In many chapters he offers specific family remedies to the problem.

Church Document

"Your Family in Cyberspace," United States Conference of Catholic Bishops, 2000. An insightful statement of the U.S. Catholic Bishops on the delights and dangers of the Internet. On-line at: www.usccb.org/comm/cyberspace.htm. Order a print version by calling 1–800–235–8722.

Magazines

Cable in the Classroom, 86 Elm Street, Peterborough, NH 03458 (www.ciconline.org). Published monthly except July and August as a guide to educational programming available on cable networks. Many cable companies buy subscriptions for local educators. Free copies and subscriptions available at 1–800–216–2225.

Entertainment Weekly, 1675 Broadway, New York, NY 10019 (www.ew.com). A magazine that looks at the whole sweep of multimedia culture: television, movies, music and books. Although the moral perspective is sometimes lacking, this is the place to go for reviews and for a broad sense of the culture.

My Friend: The Catholic Magazine for Kids. 50 Saint Paul's Avenue, Jamaica Plain, Boston MA 02130–9930 (www.pauline.org). A fun-to-read publication of information, entertainment and Christian formation for kids seven to twelve years old, including media reviews. Published by the Daughters of St. Paul monthly except July and August.

St. Anthony Messenger, 28 W. Liberty Street, Cincinnati, OH 45202 (www.AmericanCatholic.org). One of the best read general interest Catholic magazines has a strong "Entertainment Watch" column in each issue reviewing both movies and TV shows. 1–800–488–0488.

TV Guide (www.tvguide.com). The little magazine sold at supermarkets and convenience stores everywhere. It explains the premise of each show and gives the parental guidance rating, although it may not warn about adult themes and crude language.

Movies

The Vatican List

In 1995, to celebrate the hundredth anniversary of film-making, the Pontifical Council for Social Communications released a list of forty-five films the Vatican body determined to be of special merit in thee categories: religion, art and values. Some may be difficult to watch today because they are silent movies in black and white. Many of them are not for younger children. But all of them are premier examples of the filmmaker's art, well worth watching and discussing.

Religion

La Passion—Ferdinand Zecca (France, 1903)
The Passion of Joan of Arc—Carl Dreyer (France, 1928)
Monsieur Vincent—Maurice Cloche (France, 1947)
Flowers of St. France—Roberto Rossellini (Italy, 1950)
Ordet/The Word—Carl Dreyer (Denmark, 1955)
Ben-Hur—William Wyler (U.S., 1959)

Nazarin—Luis Buñel (Mexico, 1959)
The Gospel According to St. Matthew—Pasolini (Italy, 1964)
A Man for All Seasons—Fred Zinnermann (Britain, 1966)
Andrei Rublev—Andrei Tarkovsky (USSR, 1966)
The Sacrifice— Andrei Tarkovsky (Sweden/France, 1986)
The Mission—Roland Joffé (Britain, 1986)
Thérèse—Alain Cavalier (France, 1986)
Babette's Feast—Gabriel Axel (Denmark, 1987)
Francesco—(Liliana Cavani (Italy, 1988)

Art

Nosferatu—F.W. Murnau (Germany, 1922)
Metropolis—Fritz Lang (Germany, 1927)
Napoléon—Abel Gance (France, 1927)
Little Women—George Cukor (U.S., 1933)
Modern Times—Charlie Chaplin (U.S., 1936)
Grand Illusion—Jean Renoir (France, 1937)
Stagecoach—John Ford (U.S., 1939)
The Wizard of Oz—Victor Fleming (U.S., 1939)
Fantasia—Walt Disney (U.S., 1940)
Citizen Kane—Orson Welles (U.S., 1941)
The Lavender Hill Mob—Charles Crichton (Britain, 1951)
La Strada—Federico Fellini (Italy, 1954)
8 ½—Federico Fellini (Italy, 1963)
The Leopard—Luchino Visconti (Italy, 1963)
2001: A Space Odyssey—Stanley Kubrick (Britain, 1968)

Values

Intolerance—D. W. Griffith (U.S., 1916)
Open City—Roberto Rossellini (Italy, 1945)
It's a Wonderful Life—Frank Capra (U.S., 1947)
The Bicycle Thief—Vittorio Di Sica (Italy, 1948)
On the Waterfront—Elia Kazan (U.S., 1954)
The Burmese Harp—Kon Ichikawa (Japan, 1956)
Wild Strawberries—Ingmar Bergman (Sweden, 1957)
The Seventh Seal—Ingmar Bergman (Sweden, 1957)
Dorsum Uzala—Akira Kurosawa (USSR/Japan, 1975)
The Tree of Wooden Clogs—Ermanno Olmi (Italy, 1978)

Chariots of Fire—Hugh Hudson (Britain, 1981)
Gandhi—Richard Attenborough (Britain, 1982)
Au Revoir des Enfants—Louis Malle (France, 1987)
Dekalog—Krzysztok Kieslowski (Poland, 1988)
Schindler's List—Steven Spielberg (U.S., 1993)

The Experts' Favorites

The American Film Institute and the British Film Institute each created a list of the 100 Top Movies of the last 100 years to celebrate the centennial of film. The complete lists are available on-line at www.ravecentral.com/afi.html (American) and www.ravecentral.com/bfi.html (British). But here are the top five from each list (with both claiming *Lawrence of Arabia*). Unlike the Vatican list and others that follow, they are ranked in order of greatness according to the compilers:

AFI's Top Five American Films
1. *Citizen Kane* (1941)
2. *Casablanca* (1942)
3. *The Godfather* (1972)
4. *Gone With the Wind* (1939)
5. *Lawrence of Arabia* (1962)

BFI's Top Five British Films
1. *The Third Man* (1949)
2. *Brief Encounter* (1945)
3. *Lawrence of Arabia* (1962)
4. *The 39 Steps* (1935)
5. *Great Expectations* (1946)

A Thematic Approach

You do not have to be an expert or even a dedicated film buff to have favorite movies. As proof, here is a list of some of mine. I have clumped them by what I think of as religious themes, but they are also important human themes. Most of these films are easy to get at libraries and video stores, and all of them would be great starting points for family conversation.

Calling/Vocation
Chariots of Fire
Close Encounters of the Third Kind
Field of Dreams
Mr. Holland's Opus
Oh God!
On the Waterfront
The Prince of Egypt
The Sound of Music

Conversion of Heart
Entertaining Angels: The Dorothy Day Story
The Emperor's New Groove
Groundhog Day

Communion of Saints
Babette's Feast
Places in the Heart

Doubt and Faith
Shadowlands

Ethics and Evil
Citizen Kane
Schindler's List
Quiz Show

Hope
Hook
Life Is Beautiful
Shawshank Redemption (rough language)

Martyrdom/ Sacrifice
A Man for All Seasons
Casablanca
Gandhi
Romero
Star Trek II: The Wrath of Kahn

Resurrection
The Day the Earth Stood Still
E.T.
It's a Wonderful Life

Sin and Reconciliation
Cry, the Beloved Country
Dead Man Walking (not for children)
Return of the Jedi
The Spitfire Grill

Movies and Media

The following movies all demonstrate principles of media literacy described in this book or the way that people use media. Watching any of them should stimulate thought and conversation about how the mass media work, although some are definitely not for younger children:

Apollo 13 (1995, A-II, PG). The use of actual clips from television coverage of events depicted in the movie exemplifies TV as a filter of reality. The constructed nature of what results is highlighted when the networks refuse to broadcast the astronauts' program from space but later want to camp out on Astronaut Lovell's lawn when the mission goes seriously wrong.

Avalon (1990, A-I, PG). The disintegration of an immigrant family parallels their relationship with TV after its arrival in the late 1940s. They flee the dinner table to watch Uncle Miltie, then later spend a Thanksgiving eating from aptly named TV trays in front of the set. The family patriarch ends his days in a nursing home with the TV set always on.

Being There (1979, A-III, PG). Peter Sellers, as Chance the Gardener, is the original channel surfer—a man who has lived his whole life through television. "I like to watch," he says. When he is set upon by ruffians, he pulls out his remote and tries to change the channel.

Broadcast News (1987, A-IV, R). The TV news camera's

potential to lie is explored in a plot that hinges on a vacuous anchorman's false tear. The discovery of his ethical breech is a great scene, as is the producer's impassioned speech at the beginning of the movie about the dangers of tabloidism in TV news; no one listens.

Crazy People (1990, A-III, R). When a burned-out advertising executive writes ads that tell the truth, he is sent to a mental hospital. But the ads become huge hits and the executive recruits fellow patients to write more. Unfortunately, the idea is better than the movie. The best part is the outrageous ad copy about real brands.

Forrest Gump (1994, A-III, PG-13). Some of the most significant events of the Baby Boomer era—from Elvis rotating his pelvis to George Wallace standing (with Forrest Gump!) in the schoolhouse door—are seen through the prism of TV. When Gump appears on Dick Cavett's talk show, for example, it is the filmmaker's way of telling us that Forrest has become important.

The Paper (1994, A-III, R). The strains inherent in producing a daily newspaper and some of the decisions that involves are well drawn. The "budget meeting" where the editors assign an international tragedy to an inside page because no hometown residents are involved, is very believable to newspaper veterans.

The Purple Rose of Cairo (1995, A-II, PG). When a character in a Depression era romantic comedy literally walks off the silver screen and into the drab life of a New Jersey waitress, the ensuing story line offers viewers substantial material for reflection on the difference between Hollywood dreams and reality.

Sleepless in Seattle (1993, A-III, PG). This sentimental romance is primarily interesting for showing its female protagonist influenced to an extreme degree by a movie *(An Affair to Remember)* and a young boy interacting with a call-in radio show. There is also a scene in which a number of journalists compare notes on commercials, indicating the degree to which they also have become a part of popular culture.

To Die For (1995, A-IV, R). A tragicomic story of blonde ambition as a cable access "weather girl" manipulates two teenagers into killing her husband. At one point, looking straight into the camera, she says: "You're not anybody in America unless you're on TV. On TV is where we learn who we really are. What is the point of doing anything worthwhile if there is nobody watching? When people are watching, it makes you a better person."

Television Broadcast Networks

ABC Television Network
77 West 66th Street
New York, NY 10023
212–456–7777
www.abc.go.com

CBS Television Network
524 West 57th Street
New York, NY 10019
212–975–4321
www.cbs.com

Fox Broadcasting Co.
10201 West Pico Boulevard
Los Angeles, CA 90035
310–369–1000
www.foxworld.com

NBC Television Network
30 Rockefeller Plaza
New York, NY 10112
212–664–4444
www.nbc.com

Pax-TV
601 Clearwater Park Road
West Palm Beach, FL 33401
561–659–4122
www.pax.net

Public Broadcasting Service
1320 Braddock Place
Alexandria, Virginia 22314
703–739–5000
www.pbs.org

UPN Network
11800 Wilshire Boulevard
Los Angeles, CA 90025
310–575–7000
www.upn.com

WB Network
4000 Warner Boulevard
Burbank, CA 91522
818–977–5000
www.thewb.com

Web Sites

Media and Family

The Center for Media Literacy (www.medialit.org) the premier U.S. media literacy organization, selling helpful materials for parents and teachers as well as making articles available on this site.

Kaiser Family Foundation (www.kff.org) a research organization that has issued many reports about media and children, especially in the areas of sex and violence.

National Institute on Media and the Family (www.mediafamily.org) a nonprofit research and education resource for teachers, parents, community leaders and others interested in the influence of electronic media on early child-hood education, child development, academic perfor-mance, culture and violence.

National TV Turnoff Week (www.tvturnoff.org), the annual cold turkey approach to cutting down on media. The site contains many interesting statistics and persuasive articles, but has little or nothing to say about the positive contri-butions of television.

Parental Media Guide (www.parentalguide.org) a one-stop location to get descriptions of the parent advisory systems established by the movie, electronic game, music, cable and broadcast television industries.

Reasons for Movie Ratings (www.filmratings.com) a ser-vice from the Classifications and Rating Administration allowing you to search any movie by name to get both the rating and the reason for it.

Screenit.com: Entertainment Reviews for parents (www.screenit.com), a for-profit venture rating each movie on fifteen categories from alcohol/drugs to violence (minor, moderate, heavy, extreme). A click of the mouse brings up enough detailed information about each to help parents make an informed values-based decision.

Stay Safe On-Line (www.msn.staysafeonline.com), a fifteen-minute animated tutorial on Internet safety presented by Microsoft and the Boys and Girls Clubs of America. The program teaches kids and their parents to make smart choices about E-mail, chat rooms and Web sites.

U.S. Conference of Catholic Bishops Office of Film and Broadcasting (www.usccb.org/movies/index.htm), pro-viding excellent reviews of current releases, limited releases, family videos and older movies. It also gives a list of the office's ten top movies of each year since 1965.

Catholic Church

Here I offer only a few well-known sites of the estimated 1.5 million Catholic sites available. Because this is just an appetizer presented with the hope that you will explore them and learn for yourself what they have to offer, I have provided helpful categories without descriptions of each site.

Official church sites
www.vatican.va (Holy See)
www.usccb.org (United States Conference of Catholic Bishops)

Megasites
http://alaPadre.net
www.Catholic.com
www.Catholic.net
www.Catholic-usa.com
www.CatholicWeb.com

News
www.cathcom.net
www.catholicnews.com
www.catholicpress.org
www.cin.org

Spirituality
www.taize.fr
www.christdesert.org
www.christusrex.org
www.jesuit.ie/prayer
www.monks.org
www.udayton.edu/mary

Index

✗